Reviews for *Spirit Speaks*

"There is so much to understand and so much wisdom in these stories. I am inspired to write more and to ask Spirit to help me in the journey. I know I have to read these messages many more times. There is so much in them. Thank you for the inspiration."
      Kalli Dakos, Author

"This beautiful book is like a spiritual partner, part of my team supporting me and encouraging me on my own journey. Like a healing session, the words resonate within my heart. Thank you for sharing your gifts!"   Debora Gardner, Reiki Master

"The messages from Spirit in these true stories and the guidance on how to connect with Spirit are an encouragement to me to deepen and grow my spiritual life. It's good to be reminded that "there is always more." More to learn, experience, and celebrate. Thank you, Sharyn, for making this wonderful gift from Spirit available and accessible to us all."   Janet Hanna, MEd, LMT, Reiki Holy Fire III

"Wow. This book is fabulous. I loved every part of it. The interaction Sharyn had with her clients and the messages that came forth are remarkable. Not to mention, the messages from Spirit, the suggestions she gives and the exercises she shares with her readers. This is a book I will read over and over."
      Tania Yannarilli

Cover Design by Kristina Henson.

A percentage of proceeds from the sale of *Spirit Speaks*
will be donated to:

The MPS Society, a non-profit organization dedicated to supporting families affected by mucopolysaccharidoses (MPS), mucolipidoses (ML) and other related disorders; increasing professional and public awareness; and raising funds to further research into such disorders.

Hummingbird Farm, a non-profit organization, learning center, and inspirational sanctuary where animals, humans, and the earth work in partnership dedicated to deepening the understanding, respect, communication, and relationship between all living beings and the natural world around us through Animal Communication, Earth Awareness, Ceremony, and Celebration.

Consider using the Amazon Smile program to support these groups.

The author of this book offers information of a general nature regarding spiritual and emotional well-being. Techniques or activities are offered as information and do not replace the treatment or advice of your physician.

www.sharynmadison.com

SPIRIT
SPEAKS

Transformative & Healing
Messages From Spirit

Join the Conversation.

"God in All Oneness and all Identities is available,
accessible, and eager to serve humanity."

Sharyn Madison
Reiki Master & Intuitive

LIVE FROM THE LIGHT SERIES
Spirit Speaks
The Departed Speak
The Collective Speak

Dedication

To you who want to believe there is meaning to life
even when reality feels confusing, overwhelming,
and heartbreaking.

To you who are brave enough to explore
communicating between species and dimensions.

To you who are curious about Spirit Identities,
who they are, and what they offer.

To you who wonder how your departed loved ones are doing.

To you who extend effort to connect to what is beyond the physical
and visible to what is spiritual and transformational.

To you who remember we are not as limited as we have been
taught, and you seek to open the doors of intuition
and being extraordinary.

To you who in daily practice tune into Spirit,
reclaim your identity as spirit, and take ownership
of the call to be of service to raise the consciousness
on the planet, co-creating more joy for the animal,
plant, air, water, and human kingdoms.

Table of Contents

PART I: THE STORIES

PART II: HOW TO CONNECT

Spirit Speaks
Preface

Welcome to my collection of true stories highlighting Spirit messages. I celebrate that Spirit speaks to humanity with conversations that transform. Spirit, who is the collective of many identities of God, is available, accessible, and eager to help us all manifest our best life ever. Spirit wants us to be in the know, to move beyond our fears to a place of connection with our God-given Holy Resources. Whether initiated by us or them, Spirit engages in a two-way conversation giving messages that are something to behold for their perspective, wisdom, and truth. I hope you are inspired from reading **Spirit Speaks** to tap into the invisible, indescribable, yet undeniable energies of the multidimensional fields around us which are your own holy resources.

We can tap into it all because the multi-dimensions of us are designed for the multi-dimensional conversation. That is worth celebrating. We have what we need, and we can learn steps to connect for our own personal and healing conversations. I write about those steps in Part II.

In these stories, you will read how God speaks to us in many ways and through different identities called Spirit. I use the word and capitalize "Spirit" as a term for God and these collective identities of God. They angels and archangels, guardians, spirit guides, ascended masters, animal totems, departed loved ones both human and animals, and whoever my clients relate to spiritually. It is a brilliant concept of creation to fashion such a diversity of Spirit who, in collaboration with "All That Is," connects with the equally diverse personalities of humanity. Spirit works through any of these identities.

Although different in how they appear and who they call themselves, they are consistently powerful in their energetic presence. They speak gently and patiently while directly to the point because they understand us. They speak on target because they know us. They possess the unlimiting attributes of God, and yet use our limited human language to share their wisdom. All this is part of their gifts of benevolence and grace for the purposes of our highest good and highest healing.

If you are a cautious wonderer, these stories hold evidence that Spirit speaks. I realize that hearing from Spirit can seem far out there if you have never experienced it, and it can be a challenge to believe that it is true. If you have never experienced the conversation in quite this way, you may wonder if it is even safe. I questioned it all, too, until it happened indisputably for me. Now, I have heard it, seen it, felt it, and know it to be true that many identities of Spirit are with us and waiting for us to join the conversation.

As a witness, I know with unquestionable certainty that there is more to who we are than just physical beings. I see the invisible, intuitive part of us activating the circuits we have to connect with the spirit of who we are. That spirit has what it takes to reach beyond our earthbound limitations and communicate with other spiritual dimensions, the Spirit who reaches back to us. I know the conversation to be brilliant, customized, and worth seeking.

Spirit Speaks stories come from the lives of my Reiki clients and friends. They are about life situations many of us face. I started archiving the stories and the Spirit messages because I saw and felt their powerful impact. I also knew that although the messages were personalized, the guidance had a universal relevance that all of us could benefit from.

You will read about relationships, decision-making, caregiving, migraines, cancer, loss and grief. The stories are about Lou Gehrig's, addictions, overdoses, suicide, death, and the angst of it all. Then you will read the Spirit messages of inspiration and transformation with ways to cope, practical applications of insights, how to stand in love, alignment, and sacred compassion. Read and count the ways that Spirit points us all in the right direction, gives hope, and contributes insight that makes perfect sense. This combination of connecting with other dimensions and absorbing the messages produces the potential to awaken our soul. That and the restoration of our faith are only the beginnings of the transformation.

When Spirit speaks, every word has a depth of meaning so I encourage you to consider intentional reading to uncover the gold. I have italicized Spirit's words to clarify them. The stories are from true experiences so I have changed the names of my clients, their families, and their departed loved ones to respect confidentiality, and I have changed any other identifying details that might be misconstrued as clues.

Part II is a "how to" section for steps to connect. Since there are countless ways to put yourself in the vicinity of a Spirit conversation, begin by choosing what feels comfortable for you. It helps to have a basic knowledge about who Spirit is, what their language is like, and what may block the connection or enhance it. Read about channeling, therapeutic energy healing, automatic writing, and meditation. Start with one idea that resonates with you and the laundry list of ideas won't seem so overwhelming. Your own best way will fall into place. Spiritual guidance will lead you, and remember that this is a lifelong process.

It takes a lot of effort and you may go to places that are uncomfortable at first, so why would you bother? We are spiritual and multi-dimensional beings, so why not explore and experience more of who we are. These steps to connect can take us beyond the limits of our third dimensional life to experience much more. That alone is worth it.

When I look outward at the universe, there is more beyond the planet and galaxy that we see and know. When I go from the macro and look inward to the micro, there is always more to discover about cells, atoms, and sub-atomic structures. There is always more to learn about my body and spirit, more life to experience, and more miracles to witness. Modeling the expanding nature of the multiverses, there is always more: another moon, another galaxy, another mile, another pilgrimage. There is more to embrace and more yes's to possibilities. There is more of God to reach for, a deeper and wider expression of God to grasp, and an ever-expanding realm of dimensions to inherit as we embrace awakening and evolution.

As multidimensional beings, why would we not tap into all the parts of us and our world? Why not access our perceptual modes and our spiritual side in order to communicate and hear Spirit speak? When we do, we embrace the benefits of a deeper connection with ourselves and with each other including all the kingdoms of humans, beasts, plants, and the kingdoms of heaven. The more we all know and experience, the higher will be the consciousness of the planet and the universe.

I am thankful for the words and insights from Spirit given for the benefit of us all. My hope is that looking at connection with Spirit, as it happened for me and for others, will make it real and possible for you. My sacred intention is that these words will be customized by Spirit for all of us so that we receive what we need at this very moment in our lives.

In Peace, Love and Light,

Sharyn

May the gift of communication in its mysticism
become majestic in the places that it leads you, to the
inner seeds of your soul and to the outer expansions of your
outstretched arms and open heart to
embrace the Universe of Infinity.

Acknowledgments

I will be eternally grateful to my team of supporters on all sides of the veil. Their acceptance and encouragement is divine grace. All the support from my son, Jason, editing and patience from Janet, the typing and unconditional giving of my sister, Sandy, the kindness of my brothers, Blaine, and Wayne, their families, and all the love of our furry, four-legged Magrudies gives me reason to believe I have the best family ever.

The inspiration to share the messages from Spirit evolved from conversations with my friend, Sylvia. Thanks for helping me discover what I'm really trying to say. Thank you to all the editors, tech help, and reviewers: Beth, Dot, Gywn, Lisa, Kalli, Deb, Annette, Jessica, Kristina, Tania, Tina and Ruth. I am honored to have worked with so many brilliant, intuitive, and awakened family, friends, Reiki colleagues, and clients. I love this community I call Family. Love to you, Mom, on the Other Side!

Spirit Speaks
Introduction

These sacred conversations with Spirit come from my work as a professional Reiki teacher and practitioner.   You will find more information about Reiki in Part II.   Briefly, Reiki is a type of Energy Medicine which is becoming more popular as it is experienced by people who use alternative therapies to complement traditional medicine. Based on the universal and spiritual life energy called chi or ki, which is the energy that flows through all of us, Reiki makes practical application of the positive benefits of working with frequencies of energy and their effect on chi.

What I have experienced along my Reiki journey is that when the energy flows through us, there is an elevation of vibrational frequency that heals. And it strengthens the whole of who we are: body, mind, and soul.   That   healing and the consequential maturation and expansion of our perceptual modes, including our intuition, are directly related to connecting with Spirit.

We all have perceptual modes that can be developed to become more sensitized. As we allow the growth, we become acquainted with feeling more and hearing more that is outside of our usual experience. Normally, our perceptive modes are our sense of seeing, hearing, touch, taste and smell.   Those modes when enhanced are called the clairs: clairvoyance, clairaudience, clairsentience, claircognizance, clairgustance, clairsalience, clairempathy, and clairtangency.

Although some people are born further along than others in refining their perceptions, tools along the way can help any of us. Reiki is my tool. The more I experience Reiki energy, the more I land in the vicinity for receiving clear messages from Spirit and the identities of Spirit including departed loved ones. They want us to know that they are available to be of service to us. Sometimes we hear them, see them, and feel their presence, but whatever the means, they offer relevant and healing words for us. The messages can come with the strong energy of a cosmic calling or with a simple, quiet voice that lovingly whispers its anointing.

I have delivered all kinds of messages to all kinds of people and am witness to the confirmations of the truth of these life-changing conversations. As you will read, the conversations start in the intentional quietness of meditation and Reiki treatments which in effect create the safe space to invite and receive. Then I simply hear Spirit speak. What follows are the confirmations that resonate with truth, healing, and transformation that only Spirit can bring. Here are some of the stories.

Invocation to Communication With Spirit

From the Source of Light that is within
The Presence of the Spirit Identities of God,
Let Light stream into the souls of us.
Let Light descend on Earth.

From the Center of Energy that is within
The Consciousness of the Spirit Identities of God,
Let Divine purpose guide the free will and free mind of us.
Let Divinity descend on Earth.

From the Point of Love that is within
The Heart of the Spirit Identities of God,
Let Love flow into the hearts of us.
Let Love descend on Earth.

From the Collective of Healing that is within
The Will of the Spirit Identities of God,
Let Healing integrate the body of us.
Let Restoration descend on Earth.

From the planet and all of its inhabitants
Who are the Spirit Identities of God,
Let compassion saturate the experience of us.
Let Oneness restore Peace on Earth.

We are blessed to receive the healing and service
Of Light, Divinity, Love, Restoration, and Oneness.
Let gratitude lead our choices, experiences, and heart.
Letservice, compassion, and peace be our gift back to earth

PART I: THE STORIES

SECTION I: RELATIONSHIPS

Have More Fun
The Sign said, "Wow! Wow!"

"You best get it in your schedule to have a massage, Maggs, and Reiki, too. Let's release that neck and back strain, get the muscle congestion moving, and give you a chance to relax." I was talking to my friend, Maggs.

Maggs has been a teacher for nearly three decades, is still young at heart, vibrant, and loves her job. Those high school scholars love her right back. Even with all that, however, teaching takes its toll.

She came in for a Reiki treatment which is just what she needed. In the quietness, the healing energy was calming and relaxing. As I was working with the Reiki, I could tell Spirit was with us and wanting to get a discussion going. I wondered what the healing path would be. I felt led to ask her, "Do you meditate?"

She said she had tried that a couple times but hadn't made it a regular routine. She said it was too hard to slow her mind down unless it was finally time for her head to hit the pillow. Then she was out like a light until waking up, too soon, the next morning when her mind sprang out of the starting blocks to race again. "I can't get my mind to stop thinking long enough to meditate." I understood. It's hard.

Interested in the topic and happy to continue the discussion that Spirit started, I asked Maggs a short set of questions, "Do you pray? That's like meditation. Do you have a sense of Guides around you? Do you connect with a Source that you go to for help?" She replied that she does pray and is in fact very interested in finding out about her Guides.

We agreed that I would lead us through a meditation together. That could model one way to meditate. Perhaps adding meditation in her life could help her relax and let her body experience therapeutic rest and healing. From that place, maybe she could meet her Spirit Guide. So I led her in a guided meditation. I later wrote up a copy for her and you can find it here following this story.

The meditation came with ease and as our minds relaxed, it felt like we were in another space of floating yet with a calm mindfulness. The peacefulness of the experience lingered as we gradually came back to the room. We spent a few moments gently getting our feet back on the ground.

I asked Maggs how the meditation was for her, and she said she couldn't believe how relaxed she felt. She found herself intuitively connecting with the images in the meditation and had pictured each scene in her mind. She loved seeing beautiful colors and found the kaleidoscope affect delightful. She noticed and wondered why she did not see any green and blue though. She saw every color but those. Interesting.

In the meditation there was an invitation to imagine meeting Spirit Guides, and Maggs said a Being appeared and gave her a treasure chest with a gift inside. Maggs wanted to tell me what she saw in her treasure chest and said, "When I opened the treasure chest, the gift I saw was three of my favorite toys from my childhood. I didn't know what that was supposed to mean."

When you see a Spirit sign or Gift and you don't know what it means, it helps to ask yourself how did you feel at that moment. Our emotions can be clues to the meaning, a meaning which may develop in time as we contemplate it. So I asked and Maggs thought about that.

Then I shared what I had seen as an observer. I, too, saw her Guide give her a gift, and I'm smiling right now as I'm writing about it because in my vision, out from the treasure chest came a happy, bubbly squirrel.

2

It was acting like a cheerleader popping out of a jack-in-the-box toy holding up a sign with bold capital letters saying "WOW! WOW!" The squirrel was jumping up and down in the box waving this WOW sign. It looked so cute, so vivacious, excited and happy. I loved it.

I had to ask, "Maggs, do you have any idea what connection with squirrels you may have? Or why one might be enthusiastically holding up a sign saying WOW?"

At first she said, "Not a clue." But then she remembered that she in fact had noticed squirrels lately. It was unusual but she had just seen two in her yard yesterday and then again this morning. I love it when an animal unexpectedly and repeatedly crosses our path. Spirit can use animal totems, and they offer us important guidance at exactly the right time when we notice them. I said, "Go home and look up Squirrel Totem and see what it says about their message." I couldn't wait to see what the squirrel totem meant.

I also wondered why Maggs didn't see the green and blue colors. I suggested we ask Spirit right at that moment, so I did. We quieted, then I could hear clearly, *"You are carrying a Heartfelt issue that needs to be communicated. Let us help you."*

This made sense to me as green represents the heart chakra and blue represents the throat chakra which is communication of our truth. Spirit addressed it right on. I told Maggs what Spirit said and her eyes opened widely in awe. I asked her if it resonated with her, and she said she knew exactly what it meant.

What came up for her was a problem in her life that she had been struggling with for a long time. The issue boiled down to exactly what Spirit said—healing her heart and then communicating her truth. She was astonished to experience the confirmation that Spirit knew about it. And then to have Spirit say they would help. She could work with that.

I asked her if there was anything she wanted to ask Spirit before we finished. She said, "Yes, there was one more thing. Should I retire?" She was bothered by the idea that if she retired, she wouldn't know what she would do with her life. She just wanted to know if she was on the right path.

Spirit said, *"You are exactly on the right path. If you choose to retire from teaching, then do so. You have no idea what is coming next and that is by design. You need and deserve a rest period. This will be a time to not be serving others. Instead, serve you and your body with the rest that it needs. Never fear that rest times will be an end or that active service has dried up. Nada. They are simply rest times. See the time as that. Take a rest and have more fun. "*

A great note to end the session on. By the time I got home and checked my email, there was a note from Maggs. "Sharyn, the squirrel totem means to have more fun and try to take life less seriously. I am serious when I tell you this: that is exactly what I have been trying to do this school year. I am doing more with friends, I am happier, and each day I am trying to have more fun. I am truly amazed that you told me about the squirrel."

The WOW flash card the squirrel held is easy to understand. That ole' squirrel was having so much fun literally demonstrating the WOW of life which is jack-in-the-box joy. Remember the three toys Maggs saw in her box from her Guide? No doubt about it, Maggs, have some fun!

As Maggs said at the end of her email which I too say to Spirit, "Thank you for leading me on this Spiritual journey today."

SPIRIT SPEAKS: *Take a Rest and Have More Fun.*

SPIRIT SPOTLIGHT: Meditation

Science and experience agree with convincing evidence that meditation is a powerful method with many proven benefits. It can be done in a variety of ways and styles like mindfulness, guided, walking, or other movement meditations like used in Yoga and Tai Chi.

The guided meditation that I used with Maggs incorporated the valuable technique of visualization. One evidence of its positive effect is when it is used for skill development like in sports, music, and even test taking. Have you ever seen an athlete on TV rehearsing their event by using visualization?

There was a man sitting beside me on the flight from Florida to New York who spent the entire trip moving his fingers up and down on the closed computer he had on his lap as if he was playing a piano. Why was he playing an invisible piano? He volunteered the explanation. He said it worked for him to imagine a real piano under his hands. He was using an invisible keyboard to silently play the composition he would be performing at that night's Juilliard Festival in NYC.

It works because it facilitates the mind-body connection. It opens up communication between the conscious and unconscious mind as we slow down our brain. In that quiet place we can hear our inner consciousness, receive emotional and spiritual healing and have an experience with our spiritual self. We can better hear Spirit from there .

Here is the meditation that Maggs and I walked through together. This particular type of meditation uses guided imagery. Consider doing this with a partner or in a group with one person reading it because It is hard to read and visualize at the same time. Or tape record yourself reading this so you can play it back. That way you can focus more on being present for the meditation rather than the need to read.

Turn on soft music or light a candle to create a quiet mood. As with any meditation, it is helpful to begin from a place of gratitude. Think of one thing your are grateful for. Then relax into that.

MEDITATION using Guided Imagery for Meeting Your Spirit Guide

Sit comfortably, close your eyes, and take a deep breath. Breathe deeply into your abdomen. Release, relax. Once again breathe deeply, release, let go. Relax your muscles, joints, eyelids, face, neck, shoulders, hands, fingers, chest. Relax your back, legs, feet, toes. Release any pain and tension as you breathe out. Relax your whole body, mind, and thoughts. Let go of burdens, concerns, anxieties, and worries. Be present in this moment. Stay in the moment.

Become aware of the natural rhythm of your breath. Follow it in and out. Consciously breathe out any concerns you may have. Relax your mind. Feel your thoughts slowing down and drift into a more peaceful, receptive state. Relax and let go. Feel yourself surrendering to the beautiful energy flowing through you.

Now imagine yourself in a beautiful meadow. First sitting, then lying on the grass you feel the softness. Notice the smell of the grass. The smell of the earth. Plants and trees surround you. Imagine seeing and feeling the sky and clouds. The world is slowly turning. Feel the sunlight shining down on you. Feel the warmth. Breathe in the light. Breathe in the colors and healing energy of this sacred place.

Off to the right you see a path. Slowly walk down the path. It feels safe and even a bit familiar. The air is clean and the temperature is perfect. You feel comforted and nurtured by the surrounding nature. You notice the grasses blowing in the breeze, you hear the birds, and you smell the fresh air. Up ahead you notice a bench. You walk to it to sit down and rest.

While you are resting, imagine the color red. Let it wash over you. Do the same with the other colors of the rainbow. Visualize orange; let orange wash over you. Visualize yellow, then green, blue, violet, and white. Let all the colors wash over you and flow around you and through you. Breathe in the colors and imagine them cleansing you and healing you. Breathe gently in and out.

As you sit quietly, off to the left you see a Light appear. The Light is welcoming. It is soft yet beaming with radiance. It moves slowly toward you, and you decide to invite it to sit beside you. The closer it gets, the clearer is your vision, and you realize that the Light is one of your Spiritual Guides. It could be an angel, a guardian, a familiar spiritual master or a Being of Light.

You welcome your Guide just as your Guide welcomes you. The loving energy fills your heart, and you just know that your Guide has been longing to meet you and wants to communicate with you. You also want to communicate with your Guide. It feels like you have known each other for a long time. The energy feels nurturing and safe, gentle, and loving.

Then you see that your Guide is holding a treasure chest. It is closed now, and you can see it is covered with jewels and gold. Your Guide graciously hands the chest to you, and you know you may open it. There is a gift inside for you. It might be an object, or an animal. It might be a feeling, simply a word or a promise. It is a special gift for you and has meaning.

Look inside. What is in the chest? You see what it is, and you feel grateful. Take a moment to hear and know what the meaning of the gift is.

If you have any questions about the gift, or any questions at all, ask your Guide now. Enjoy and appreciate the energy of the gift and of the presence of your Guide.

Tuck your gift in your heart for safe keeping. When you are ready, thank your Guide for meeting with you. You know that your Guide is always available and will always be with you. You know that you can meet again with your Guide any time that you want to.

Your Guide will smile in agreement and in satisfaction that they have had this time with you. Then watch as your Guide gently moves away and watch the Light fade across the meadow. Bless them in namaste and know that Spirit loves you deeply and is eager to meet with you again soon.

Rise up from the bench and walk back up the pathway into the meadow. You enjoy the colors of nature, the soft sounds, and the refreshing smells as you go.

Imagine yourself relaxed and peaceful. The energy of the experience feels cleansing, healing, soothing and transforming. Breathe it in and out, again in and out. One last gentle breath and you are ready to come back into the room. Open your eyes. Notice the room, the sound around you now, and notice your body. Wiggle your toes and gently shake your hands. Take whatever time you need to feel your feet back in your shoes.

Here is a message from Spirit:

Dear Beloved, This is a message for you to honor your communication with us. We honor the chance to be three dimensional with you. The soul in you is the seed of potential. Thank you for your willingness to give your soul what it needs and wants which is attention from you and the opportunity to be free without the weight of concerns, free because everything really is taken care of.

Thank you for your hard work and all you accomplish. Enjoy the work because you can. Also enjoy the non-work moments because you can. Watch for hearts today, our three dimensional symbol for honoring you. Like a treasure hunt, be delighted.   Love, Spirit

Post It
Who is taking your power?

Patsy called and said, "I have to cancel my appointment. I'm covered with hives." "Oh dear," I said. "We'll reschedule when you are feeling better." I cancelled the appointment, re-opened 4:00 in my schedule and went on with my day. It was 3:55 when Patsy called back. "Is there any chance I could come in now? My hives have calmed down." The time was open, just as it was meant to be.

As soon as she came through the door she expressed her upset. "What's with these hives? They come and go at will. I've been to the doctor and we can't figure out what is causing them. I've taken different medicines and the hives keep coming back. I'm a teacher and I just can't go to school with hives all over my face!"

We worked through the possible scenarios that could cause hives like a food allergy, a reaction to medication or body soap. Have you changed laundry detergent? Your diet? Have you installed new carpeting? Painted your house? How is your stress level? Are you exercising?

We did muscle testing, also known as applied kinesiology, to check further for other potential causes. Is Patsy allergic to soy? Dairy? Clams? Shellfish? Or peanuts?

"Well, let's get started with your treatment." As always, I invited our Guides to be present and any other Ascended Beings who could come and help us for guidance and healing.

I immediately heard, *"Check her chakras."* I often do that with the Reiki treatments so nothing unusual there. I briefly introduced Patsy to chakras and how they can be indicators of illness and can influence healing. The best scenario for health is to have chakra energy movement which feels open and free-flowing as opposed to dense and closed. After asking her permission to check hers, I began an energy assessment using my hands in an above-the-body quiet sweep to check energy flow and balance around each major chakra.

The chakra system was almost completely shut down. Only the sixth chakra, known as the third eye, showed movement, so I knew this center of intuition could be helpful. I said to Patsy, "Our best resource at the moment is your intuition. Intuitively, what do you think is causing the hives?" Her immediate answer was stress.

Applying the Reiki with that in mind, I felt the energy flowing like a tingling and pulsating in my hands as as vibration with heat. Moving along the chakras and energy lines, I noticed that wherever I placed my hands, I kept seeing the color yellow. Bright yellow. In chakra work, yellow represents the solar plexus chakra, the self-power center. So after the initial full body Reiki work, I went back to the solar plexus to focus more Reiki there.

Thinking about this chakra and self-power, I heard Spirit say, *"Ask her WHO is taking her power."* Then the color shifted to red, the color of the Root Chakra which references "family," so I knew that she was giving her power away to someone in her family.

Before I said anything, I felt like I needed a little more information, so I continued giving Reiki around her ears and throat. The energy buzz really kicked up so I stayed there with my hands, paused to focus, and listened. I heard from Spirit who said, *"Ask her WHO is not hearing her."* I moved down to her throat chakra which represents the strength to talk, to communicate, and to speak our truth. Spirit spoke again, *"She feels that she is not allowed to say her truth."*

Taking the lead from Spirit, now I started a conversation with Patsy by asking "WHO is taking your power?" Patsy was very quiet. Letting her reflect a free moments, I gently continued. "WHO is not hearing you? Who is not letting you say your truth? Who are you letting take your power which leaves you unable to speak your truth peacefully?"

Now Patsy was ready for a conversation. She immediately said, "I can tell you WHO. It's my husband. I HATE the job that he has, and he doesn't listen to me. I want him to quit! I leave him post-it notes all over the house telling him how I feel about it."

A Pandora's box opened and Patsy had lots to say. There was plenty here to cause stress and hives. I silently asked our Guides, "Which way do you want to go with this?" Wonderfully loving and gentle, here is the wisdom given from Spirit:

We would love for Patsy to be free to speak her truth. Because she likes lists and practical approaches, here are things she could try:

First, say your truth in a different way. The post-it notes aren't working. Is there a different way you could say what you need to say? Could you talk about your truth face to face?

Secondly, say your truth in a different place—literally—like outside of your house instead of inside, or in the living room rather than the bedroom, the kitchen rather than the car.

Thirdly, say your truth from a different place—figuratively—like from your heart instead of your head. Could you use compassionate words instead of judging words, or kind words instead of angry words? Seek to use understanding words instead of words coming from the place of hurt and the place of your desperation from being misunderstood and not heard. That will open the space to be heard.

Lastly, let him have his own journey. You hate his job. Does he? How does he feel about it? This job just may be perfect for him to learn

11

what he is here to learn and to experience what he needs and wants to experience.

How can you be in a relationship with him and still let him have his separate journey? You can have a relationship being together as friends, partners, and lovers and STILL let him have HIS journey. His journey need not be a reflection on you, who you are, or what your life lessons are. Being together is about support. It is the resistance and disallowing that causes separation, not his job. It is the anger and resentment that causes distance between you, not his job. In contrast, it will become the allowing and the understanding that will empower your relationship and reduce your stress. Think on these things.

There is nothing like the strength of personal power that enables you to love yourself and love others unconditionally. What a gift to give, giving freedom to others for their personal journeys with all the consequences that could bring learning and evolution.

SPIRIT SPEAKS: *Who are you empowering with your love and compassion? Who are you letting have their own journey?*

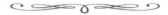

SPIRIT SPOTLIGHT: Balancing Chakras For Personal Power

Chakras are part of our energy anatomy. It is an entire system which supports the chi that all living things have, chi being the life energy. There are three major parts:

Meridians: energy pathways beneath the surface of the skin that supply chi or life energy to our organs and tissues; similar to our circulatory system

Auras: the multilayered field of energy surrounding the body

Chakras: energy centers; "spinning wheels" that draw energy in and out of the body

We all have seven major chakras each having a different characteristic, function and responsibility in the body, and all of them having the major purpose of taking in chi from around us and transmuting it into various frequencies that our subtle energy system needs. The transmuted chi energy then travels from the chakras to our biological systems, organs, tissues, and cells.

The system gets sluggish when chakras get blocked, out of balance, chronically stagnate or overloaded. Blocks can be caused by illness, stress, injury, or over-tiredness. Whatever the reason, the blocked chakra is like having a kink in the hose of the energy flow resulting in a weakness that could manifest as illness, or on other levels like a lack of energy, difficulty concentrating, lack of motivation, or difficulty communicating, all depending on which chakras are affected.

It's a good idea to pay attention to your chakras and keep them open and balanced to enable the energy to flow freely through your entire body for optimal healing and good health. Balancing chakras is important for your overall well-being. You can ask an energy medicine practitioner for help to balance your chakras, or you can do so yourself. One tool that helps me is self-Reiki. Any of the Reiki techniques are helpful when you use them on yourself, especially the grounding, hand placements, and meditations.

For this spotlight, we are focusing on the universal theme of Patsy's story: feeling accepted and heard.   Here are Spirit recommended techniques for strengthening personal power and grounded in your truth which are most closely connected to the solar plexus, throat, and heart chakras:

• Let yourself be involved in creativity. Is there something creative that you love doing? Allow yourself time to create. The color of your sacral chakra and creativity is orange so visualize orange, wear orange, eat orange food, bounce an orange ball.

• Do the same for your solar plexus which is your center of personal power. Immerse yourself in the frequency of yellow. Do the same for your heart which is green.

• Strengthen and open any chakra by breathing through that chakra. Practicing breathing through your heart chakra. As you breathe through your nose, imagine pulling in and "breathing" in Light and Love through your heart. Then as you exhale, imagine your breath going back out through your heart. Do the same through whatever chakra you are working on. Imagine it going through your back as well encompassing all of you, filtrating through the front and back.

• During your meditation or at other times throughout the day, put your right hand over your left hand, on the chakra that you are focusing on. That loving touch helps you focus on that area and can be effective in getting the energy moving there.

• Imagine your chakras breathing a sigh of relief that you were giving them permission to be open to let life energy flow freely in and through them. You will have optimal health and well-being when all the chakras are open and functioning.

• Focus on your chakras during your meditation. Do and say the following:

Quiet your mind and visualize yellow. Let the solar plexus chakra color of yellow wash over you as it strengthens your confidence in who you are and your knowing that Life itself and the Power of God supports you. Say to yourself, "I am the power of Love and Light and I express my power peacefully. I am at home and at peace with my power. My power is not threatening to others. I use my power to meet my challenges, not to struggle and resist but to do hard things, lean into difficult feelings, and rise above them and succeed in moving forward. I believe in myself. As I go out in the world and reach out to the world with my power, I will help to make a difference in the world by giving it Love and Light."

Visualize green. Let the heart chakra color green wash over you as it strengthens your belief in love and heals the inner wounds of pain and hurt. Say to yourself, "I am grateful. I am kind, loving, and good to myself and others. I can allow my heart to heal and to heal me so that I can be of service to others. I am God's expression of Love on this earth. I let love, peace, and joy permeate me, guide me and inspire me to give out the energy of the heart."

Visualize blue. Let the throat chakra color blue wash over you as it strengthens your conviction of your truth. Say to yourself, "I express my truth peacefully, confidently, and in accordance with my surrender to my Higher Self. I can speak my truth because it is MY truth, from my heart, and I can speak it without demanding that MY truth is the only truth. I honor others as they speak their truth. I am honest, trustworthy, and willing to be a Light of Goodness and Hope."

Our wish is for you to always know unconditional love.
While that may not be possible on the earth plane
for every moment of your earth experience, it will be possible
for every moment of your experience with your Guides.

Shall I Just Call It Quits?
What comes next could be from your Higher Self.

"I am so stressed. It's my boyfriend, Mitch," Esther said. "I don't know if I should take this relationship any further. He complains that I'm never available for time for him. But I have my daughter and all her activities, I'm trying to take care of the rental house as well as my own house, I have my job, and then there is the constant organizing of the grocery list, laundry, researching the new car I need…he just doesn't understand. Should I just call it quits?"

I am glad that Esther gets Reiki treatments to help her calm down, and in that state of relaxation, her thinking can settle and make room for clarity. The calming allows space for hearing guidance from the spirit of our Higher Selves, Guides, and Guardians from the Other Side. In Esther's case, it was the spirit of her departed father who offered loving advice. Read his practical problem-solving steps personalized for Esther, a step-by-step approach perfect for her personality. They are helpful for any relationship that is stretched to the limits due to chores, responsibilities, and the stuff of life that robs us of our joy if we let it.

How To Manage Life's Overwhelms from Esther's Father

Step 1: Get a pencil and paper and do this.

• *Fill in the blank: "In order to be more available, I need to get these things done first: _____."*

This will become a list of all the things you need to do around the house and other responsibilities that you feel you need to get done before you can be available for anything else.

• *Prioritize the list. Number them in order of what's most important to get done first or regularly. Don't forget to include time just for you.*

• *Then say: "Here is the compromise that I am willing to make: If you help me take care of the top 3, I will let go of the bottom 3 in order to have more time to devote to you and our relationship."*

Step 2: Ask yourself: How do you feel about letting Mitch do some of the child-rearing?

Let go and let him do some of the care-taking. If you can't trust him, is it about who he is or about who you are? It could be really good for the both of them and for you, a win/win/win.

Step 3: From our perspective, chores and things are not as important as relationships.

Ask yourself:
• *If this was your last day on Earth, what would you want to do with your time?*
• *If this was their last day, and let's say they didn't know it, what would you want to do with their time?*
• *What would you regret if they had to leave without notice?*
  Use this to decide how you are going to spend your day's worth of energy and time.

Step 4: Develop a question and journal about it.

• *Develop a question from your issue or concern.*
For example, If you see you aren't having enough time for you, then ask: "How can I make time for things I want to do?" If you see that preparing the meals is taking up a lot of time, then ask: "What is a better way to plan meals so that it doesn't take me so long?" If you see that your job is causing undue exhaustion, then ask: "Ten years from now, is this the job that I want to be doing every day?"

• *Journal about it, ask the questions you came up with and seek wisdom from your Higher Self, your Spirit Guides or your guardians like me. Let's say "Spirit."*

In journaling you will be guided. Spirit can touch your thinking while you journal. The act of writing separates out your conscious mind from your subconscious. Within that gap there is room for Spirit to initiate thoughts in your subconscious. There is space for silence so you can hear Spirit speak. It may seem like you are just writing what comes next in your mind. That's good because what comes next could be from your Higher Self, Spirit.

Step 5: Look at your day through your heart, not your fear or worries.

As your heart leads, think about things you are grateful for, that you love and enjoy. Begin your day with thinking about the positive things it will bring. The gratitude that will flow from your heart has the power to dissipate a fear, minimize a worry, and clear a path to what will touch your heart the most which is love and joy.

SPIRIT SPEAKS: *Look at your day through your heart, not your fears or worries.*

SPIRIT SPOTLIGHT: Journaling For Relief And Clarity

Journaling is a favorite tool of mine for connecting with Spirit. Even if you only write for a few minutes, the benefits are worth the effort. If this is a new technique for you, it may seem odd at first. Keep up with it though and enjoy the personal time for yourself. Just start writing honestly. Express yourself whether in scribbles or mad lines, circles or pensive doodles.

If you can't think of anything to write, write that. Or draw that. What does it feel like or look like to not have anything to say? Or take time to contemplate questions you may have and write those down.   Write about or draw where you would rather be than where you are. Focus on your heart as best as you can. If it's a list that you need to write down to un-clutter your mind, then by all means get the thinking out on paper so you can better drop down into your heart.

Here's a trick to help you get in touch with your heart and even your subconscious: Write or draw using your non-dominant hand.   It's surprising what comes out.

Draw a box. Put in it whatever you want to let go of. Let it be a sacred gift to let go of feelings, situations, people, things. It's surprising what goes in, and surprising what you can let go of.

Journaling For Answers
At the end of Part II in this book I write more about Automatic Writing. For now, after clearing out and letting go, you may decide you want to journal for answers.   Clarify your intention to ask for help. Intend to be open to receive. Humbly approach the act of writing as a sacred time to meet with the spiritual side of you, your God, or whatever identity of God you feel most connected to. Write your heart-felt question, let your pen rest for a moment, then pick it back up and start writing again. Write whatever you hear, one word at a time.

It might look like this: "Dear God, This is Sharyn here. I'm not feeling so great today. I'd like to ask for your guidance. What wisdom would you share with me about ...."

Over time, your discoveries may include more effective ways to word the questions, how to bring more quietness to your space, and what the language of Spirit sounds like. Confidence in your hearing will rise, and you will experience more ease in the process and in the believing and trusting that those words on that paper are from Spirit. You will read back what you wrote and be floored by the truths and targeted answers, the resonance you feel in your heart, and the beautifully stated wisdom that you know didn't come from just you.

Watch for journaling to become helpful for what it gives back. Feel the relief in the honesty that emerges and the diffusion of the depression, anger, grief, and anxiety. Be consoled by the freedom in releasing your feelings without the fear of being exposed or of losing. Find comfort in the feeling of acceptance that surprisingly surfaces out of the jumble of emotions. It's a practice I highly recommend for the peace it brings to your mind and soul.

"Strength and courage are a team.
Just remember that strength is not about
bucking up, working hard or being strong willed.
Real strength is in the peace that passes all understanding."

There are good times, and then there are...Family Times
Stand in the Love and the vibration of Love.

Many clients come in with countless variations of troubles within the family. Most often it's the biological family but the same situations occur in our adopted or outside family groups like friends, neighbors, or colleagues at work. Either way, when the troubles end up as lawsuits, that's mostly about money. When the troubles become demands that one partner "gets out of my house," it's about hurt feelings. Fights often boil down to misunderstandings and missed opportunities for healthy communication.

There can be times of tragic loss, whether the loss is a job, a home, or a loved one, and people end up accusing, blaming, and stealing what they feel belongs to them. The grief becomes more about an exaggerated fiction, or may end us as using property or children or grandchildren as chess pieces in the game of power. Siblings stop talking to each other, partners shut the door or walk out, relatives rage and the drama reigns on.

Less aggressive but equally annoying and destructive over time are the family times when one person feels like they are doing all the giving. It's when things feel one-sided with non-ending care-taking, tireless and unappreciated work to keep things together, and constant giving, giving, giving. It's stressful around the partner who loses their job and plays golf all day rather than cook dinner, do the laundry, or look for a job. Or the kin who comes and goes, or worse yet stays with never a thought to give back. All countless expressions of Family Times, the good and the challenging.

A client came in for Reiki, distressed by much of the same trouble. From her perspective, her partner was headed down the tubes for his lack of effort to share in the chores of the household, his non-existent appreciation for her working all day while he stayed home, and his total unavailability for any kind of support. I could feel her stress.

I began the Reiki treatment and half way through, I saw a vision of a bird's nest with a mother bird and baby bird in it. The perspective I had was looking down on the nest nuzzled right in the fork of two strong branches, the picture of peace. My vision expanded as I backed up from that vantage point, and I could see that behind the nest was a raging waterfall, a torrent of water crashing over the precipice. Talk about a picture of peace. How astounding, the perfect trust in the nest and in the strength of the tree with no apparent fear about the thundering water running right beneath it. Remarkable.

I began to wonder. I saw no father bird in the picture so I wondered where he was. I wondered if he proudly built the nest for the mother and was off finding food. Or perhaps, oh dear, what if he built the nest in a hurry and didn't think about the nest being in a dangerous spot. Perhaps mother bird said, "What the hell were you thinking???" Unappreciated, he left.

Suddenly, the vision disappeared as did my speculations. Out of nowhere the feelings of the presence of energy disappeared as well. The room felt empty. I could sense no vibration, no sacred presence, no Reiki, no heat...what was happening?

I heard Spirit say, *"What do you feel?"* I said, "I feel like I don't like this. There's a vacancy, a void, an emptiness. I don't like it at all."

As if to fill up the void, in rushed thoughts and feelings of worry, fear, questions, and old tapes of not being worthy or good enough. What happened? What's going on?

This is for your client, for the help in understanding her situation. Explain that this is what her partner is feeling. Vacancy. Void. Empty. Then worried, afraid, unworthy. Feel that. Understand that.

With understanding comes compassion. It could be worth the effort to see from that different perspective. What if you could trust the branches, trust the nest? What if you could not? Could it be helpful to know that there is void, sorrow, loss, and lack of confidence for the partner more so than what seems like not caring, not being responsible, or not trying? Do you feel the difference?

We offer free will to humanity. You get to choose understanding and compassion, or not. Your partner gets to choose vacancy, void, or not. In time, you or your partner may want to heal and change. They may want to see live differently and not rob anyone else of their Light. They may even ask for help while on bended knee for Light to guide their path. Or not. That is choice. What is your choice of Light to offer them or others?

We completed the session on a positive note as Spirit filled up the room again with healing and love. It was such a wonderful gift to feel it and absorb it. Later, as I gathered my things in the office, I recalled my wondering about the question, "What if a person's partner doesn't want to change? It could be so hard to live day after day with that." I looked down at the day's calendar and read a quote from the Dalai Lama: "... look at your problem person and thank them for helping you get closer to your Buddha-hood."

We cannot control another. Their choices may affect us greatly, and it is not easy to let others have their own journey when the paths cross and their choices affect ours. Will it bring out our Buddha-hood? Or the best of our higher self? Or perhaps even the part that needs to be healed or transformed?

I remembered a client who came in distraught and crushed in spirit because her son and daughter-in-law would not allow her to see her grandchildren because of a family spat. How does one survive that? Spirit reminded us of this:

The best option is to stand in love. Keep loving your grandchildren from where you are even though it is at a distance. The "distance" will disappear when it comes to your love. They will know and feel the vibration of your love. Even in their sleeping and dream state they will feel and know the power of your pillar of Light and Love. The vibration of love has no boundaries nor is held back by any restrictions. And don't worry about losing time by not being able to see them. You have forever to love them.

SPIRIT SPEAKS: *Stand in the Love.*

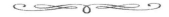

SPIRIT SPOTLIGHT: How To Stand In The Love.

A family member came in for Reiki because she was under tremendous pressure from siblings who since their mom died were fighting over the inheritance or better explained, the lack of inheritance. In aggressive anger they refused to talk to my client anymore. She was so distraught about the terrible mess and asked, "Will we ever be speaking again?" She said she felt alone, out-ranked, confused, and misunderstood. Open to guidance, we invited the spirit of her departed mom to help.

Oddly, I kept hearing a cricket sound. Then her departed mom said, *"I know what it's like to feel small under the influence of your siblings. I often felt like a cricket, small but I could be loud at least under the cover of darkness."*

My client's eyes popped with resonance. Aww, the meaning of the cricket sound. The surprising image of the cricket for my client had her own resonance. She had just dealt with a cricket that morning in the barn. What are the chances? That confirmation brought the relief of understanding that her mom really knew how it was to feel small in the fray of family affairs.

Her mom continued with practical advice. "Wear the bracelet I left for you. Let it remind you of the circle of life and that it all comes back to the circle of love. Wear it every day. Look at it to remind you to let go of them and their drama. For yourself, stand in the circle of love."

How can you let go when family brings trauma into your life?

1. Remember it is their path, their journey. You can walk tall in your own yet still love them.

2. When feeling sad, spend effort creating for yourself a new family with the people you love to be around. Family doesn't have to be biological to be family. Let sadness become the energy you need to reach out.

3. Work on your grounding. That helps for centering that gives strength for standing in love. It gives you the courage to let them have their own journey while you create and navigate yours.

4. To Ground: Strengthen your root chakra by wearing red, or bringing something red into your home. Imagine your feet standing on solid ground. Let them sink into the floor. Feel them holding firm to the earth as if you had powerful magnets on your feet. Imagine roots growing from your feet into the earth. Breathe through your feet. Stay there until you feel like no one can push you over.

5. If there are deep wounds to be healed, imagine removing the attack arrows from your heart. Ask for help from Archangel Michael. Imagine Archangel Raphael filling the wounds with warm, healing oil. Ask for help to protect you from any new attacks.

6. When you hear negative words or thoughts, acknowledge them. Say thank you, then let go and refuse to think them anymore. Replace them with gratitude and love thoughts even if the best thing you can think of is "Thank you for helping me get closer to my Buddha-hood."

7. When you are ready, reach for the higher vibration of understanding. Understanding invokes forgiveness for the peace that it will give you. It's a choice you can make. If you have no idea why people are acting like they are, chances are they are living in fear and from a place of fear rather than a place of love. Expand your circle of love to reach out to them. That vibration will be there to offer them ways to break their cycle of fear. In times when you do not have the strength to send them healing love, you can always pray and ask for help from your spiritual team and their spiritual team. Along with the power of understanding, use the power of gratitude for the grace that it manifests.

You are working, shining, and electrifying.
We are sourcing, providing, and beaming with joy and pride.
We will never let you go, never leave your side, and always have your back. We will always hold your feet, re-fill your heart, energize your thoughts, and always be available for more than you can think or imagine.

Dearest Beloved, your Light will shine brightest when plugged into our Source. Visualize yourself at your recharging station.

SECTION II: DECISIONS

That Settles It

Believe what you hear when your heart confirms it.

Tanya had come in for an appointment at her wit's end. She told me that these last three weeks had been the most horrible ever. She had to make a really big decision, and she did not want to talk about it. Her stress was over the top, and she knows she is doing it to herself, digging a hole deeper and deeper by spinning her wheels, but what can she do? She hears voices in her head but has no clue about which one to listen to, or if she should listen to ANY of them. Her countenance clued me in to the seriousness of her status.

Tanya was facing what many of us face, needing to make what we perceive as a huge decision and just not having a clue which way to go. With all the voices competing for the upper hand, which ones should we believe or follow? When we ask for spiritual help, how do we know that what we think we are hearing is really guidance from Spirit and not just us making something up?

Our goals for the Reiki treatment were to help Tanya relax and clear her mind by opening and balancing her chakras so that she would have full access to herself, her common sense, and good judgment. We wanted to help her feel grounded and have clarity.

We started the treatment, and I channeled Reiki energy to all the chakras. Before long, I heard a message from her Guide who identified himself as Archangel Michael. *"Don't believe what you hear."* It was a confident message followed by a presence of compassionate love. The message continued with *"Don't believe what you hear unless your heart confirms it. When your heart confirms it, you are hearing your message of truth and guidance. There is centeredness and help for you from being in nature. Go outside, be with nature. There experience grounding. Being in nature is not just for moving around. Be outside, be very still, and listen."*

I shared the Spirit message with Tanya, and from her countenance it appeared that the messages had great meaning and brought her immediate peace and resolution. Once again Spirit had given the exact message that was needed.

"Wow", she said, "I know what is the truth now. That settles it. It's a new concept to me, listening to my heart, but I feel it. And yes, I will get outside, spend time in nature, and listen."

I thought about the fact that many of us experience torment about decisions. We ask, "How do I know the truth about what I hear and the truth about decisions I need to make?" As Tanya and I talked a little more, we realized together that one reason we lose touch with our heart is the fear. We can have such a fear about making the wrong decision that we become blocked and paralyzed.

Archangel Michael was still with us and I could hear him say *"Don't be afraid that you will make a wrong decision. Whatever decision you make, I will always be with you. There is no judgment here. There is no punishment, only correction if needed. You will continue to learn how to connect with your heart. It is a journey."*

SPIRIT SPEAKS: *Whatever decision you make, I will always be with you.*

There is no judgment here.
There is no punishment; only correction.

28

SPIRIT SPOTLIGHT: Decision-Making

Decision-making is a daily event, some more far-reaching than others. Is there a formula for how to make the right one? Spirit is always happy to assist. Spirit is pleased to be available to help with guidance. Here are some ways to help with decision-making.

1. Saying "no" is an option when needed. Never fear by saying no that you will miss an opportunity. You will always attract more and Spirit is always looking out for your best interest by bringing more.
Saying no never excludes the gift of tomorrow and the many gifts to come in such as opportunities, blessings, and experiences.

2. You can best tolerate the situation of not knowing what to do by first of all focusing on grounding. Grow roots and stand tall. Use tools for additional support such as creating a sacred space for your own renewal, use aromatherapy and crystals, get a Reiki treatment or a massage, spend time with friends, or take naps. In time your guidance will come as will your clarity.

3. While waiting for guidance, bloom where you are planted believing in what attracted you there for the purposes of your joy, growth, or service. It is easier to make decisions from this place of stability than from a place of exhaustion or burnout, discouragement or loss of confidence.

4. *Sort out the fears from the feelings of the heart. The heart knows more than you might realize for making your best decisions. How do you sort out fears? We suggest searching your feelings and thoughts. List them, acknowledge them, and ask, "Which ones are based in fear?" Let those go and see what is left.*

Then ask, what does the heart say? "I'm excited, honored, blessed, and love that I can do this work?" Or does it say, "what I really want right now is rest peace, restoration, and time to do other things."

5. Practice the traditional list-making of pros and cons. Ask for help to see the third alternative that you are missing, the one thing that is less obvious, the piece that Spirit would see from Spirit's perspective.

6. Ask for a Sign if you wish. Remember the story of Gideon and the fleece? Wanting to be sure, he asked for more than one sign. That's OK too. See what all lines up while you maintain an attitude of authentically wanting guidance, appreciating holy help, and asking for the resonance of peace to come with the sign. Then watch for it.

7. Use the Magic Word technique. Think of a word you would not hear in the average conversation, and give it a meaning to your situation like "Moonshine" means yes. "Declaration of Independence" means no. Then listen for the word to magically pop up in conversation.

8. Oprah offers an interesting technique. She calls it the Placemat method. Use paper the size of a placemat, fold it in half, and on one side write down the list of what is your responsibility and on the other side list what is the Universe's responsibility.

Remember it is all right to take a rest from Service
so that you may fill up your soul.
We will always be with you. We want you to be happy and
fulfilled so take the path of peace and joy.

9. Many decisions boil down to money. Is the fear of the lack of money a big piece of the picture? Totally understandable since in terms of essential it is right up there with oxygen, right? Well, Spirit never wants us to worry about money.

Abundance, Divine Compensation, and Manifesting are all topics worthy of full discussion. For now, consider asking yourself this question: "If money was no object, what would you choose to do?"

10. What part of the decision holds something you may regret the most down the road?

11. Most importantly, what fills you up? When you discover what fills you up, what it is that you could do all day without realizing that time is passing, then that is your purpose. Focusing on what will take you there is worth the choosing.

Spirit says, *"Life is your Treasure Hunt with trails and clues and discoveries galore. Enjoy the journey as the destination is the Beyond."* There are many decisions and choices for the discoveries of fulfillment, and they will all lead to the same glorious destination which is the Beyond. What could be more glorious than that?

12. Whatever we decide as the path, we will still get to the destination. We might as well let go of the struggle and enjoy more of the journey.

"Focus your gifts and talents by first considering what
pleases you not only as you seek to grow with practice
and in wisdom but also as you seek to serve.
What pleases you? Bloom there.

In the meantime, enjoy your expansion and rest
in the quiet times. Rest without alarm or worry that you
are somehow not in the right place. Rest is a gift for you."

Love, Beau & Shadrack
Tell her we're here!

When Angela walked in, I could see that she looked worn out. She said she was having quite a time caring for her elderly mom who was having a number of really tough medical issues. Her mom, Lydia, had a stroke and was able to move about but was not able to verbally communicate at all. Plus her mom was not eating because of constant pain in her stomach, and she was losing weight rapidly. Lydia let her daughter know for certain that even with all the problems, she was not going to any rehab or nursing facility!

I could tell from Angela's countenance that she was exhausted from the efforts. The care-taking role was a difficult path, and she was doing it alone. Tragically, her husband had passed not too long ago so now she was working full-time, taking care of the house and barn, taking care of her horse, taking care of her mom, and life was overwhelming.

As she talked, I could hear that Angela felt overcome by everything. I knew she needed a reprieve. I was glad she had come in for a treatment. We invited our Guides and asked for a healing for Angela's highest good. In the quietness of the Reiki, I could feel the energy of a soul presence from, well, I didn't know. They are calling themselves her beloved horses.

I was not expecting that so I asked again, "Who are you?" Excited as could be, they told me again, *"We're here! We're Angela's beloved horses! Tell her that we're here!"*

Horses talk? Besides, I thought Angela only had one horse so I was confused. "I'm perplexed here—enlighten me please. Who are you again?" Politely, one energy stepped forward. He identified himself as Angela's horse.

"I died," he said, *"and now I spend time as spirit in the pasture. I'm here for Angela. I'm always in the pasture with her,"* he continued. *"I could increase my vibration and go to a higher place, but I want to spend time here in the pasture. I know Angela needs me. So I'm here."*

I could feel the love. The energy that filled the room from this horse radiated with such joy. I could feel their excitement and anticipation to be making contact with Angela. *"Please tell her that I'm in the pasture for her!"* I remembered that Angela had said that she was concerned about her horse needing a buddy, friend and companion so I decided to ask the horse, since he was in the pasture, if he was helping Angela's new horse. He said, *"I will if Angela asks me to."*

I needed some kind of validation because this was outside the box. We had asked for help for Angela's highest healing, but I really wasn't expecting it to come like this. Before I could get another question out, a different horse energy stepped forward asking for time to talk. I said, "Sure. Who are YOU?"

"I'm Angela's other horse!"

I said, "Nice. I'm impressed that you are here, surprised actually. Could you do me a favor? I need validation for Angela. Can you give me something? How about tell me your name."
The horse said, *"Jimbo."*

I wondered if I had heard that correctly. That's an odd name for a horse. So I asked, "Did I hear that right? Jimbo? Is that a nickname or your real name?" I saw the letters in all caps: BEAU. I needed to clarify so I asked, "Beau? Are you Jimbo also known as Beau?

The horse answered, *"Yes, my name is Beau and it means handsome. I'm a really handsome horse."*

I smiled. I loved the energy of these horses. Next I asked, "Do you have a specific message you want me to give Angela?"

"Tell her that the only responsibility she has with her Mother is to feed her. Nothing else. That's it. The rest is all her Mom's journey."

Now that was to the point, quite powerful really. To clarify, I asked Beau, "What I'm feeling is that you want Angela to be able to let go and have relief from this enormous task of care-taking, is that right? That all she has to do is feed her mom and not take on everything else? She doesn't need to find an answer for everything or solve all the problems because many of the pieces are up to her mom to figure out? She can let go and let her mom have her own journey? Is this what you are saying?"

"Yes. Tell her to just feed her. Angela does a good job at that. That's the bottom line of what her mom needs now. Nutrition. Period. Then you'll have energy to better feed her soul." I liked the resolution in that. Something obviously had to give for Angela, maybe this was the answer.

I decided to check in with Angela and let her know what was going on, so I quietly said, " Two horses are here with their lovely energies to talk to you. One horse said he has already passed some time ago, but he stays in the pasture for you. Does this mean anything to you?"

"Oh my gosh," she exclaimed, "You mean Shadrack. I miss him so much!" She told me the story about her beloved horse and how his death had absolutely broken her heart. She was clearly touched to hear from him. As she cried she said they were tears of joy to hear that he was still with her in spirit and that he was in the pasture. She said it felt so amazing and so healing. She was crying and beaming at the same time.

Then I told Angela that another horse was with Shadrack. "He said his name is Jimbo, also known as Beau."

"Yes, Beau. How would you ever know that name???"

"Well, that's what he said." Angela went on to explain, "Beau is my winning racehorse and is indeed handsome. Very handsome. He came originally from Mississippi so his name was Jimbo. When he came to New York, he was renamed Beau. Wow, I can't believe you knew that name."

I told Angela that Beau had a message for her about her mother. I shared the message, and she said that made complete sense to her. She could feel relief already just considering the idea. She said that it felt like she was granted permission to back off from all the effort that had become so much that she couldn't find a way out from under it until —until hearing this message from Beau.

We talked about it more asking out loud, "What would happen if she didn't have to do everything? What if she was truly honest about what she could do and not do? What if she started taking care of herself? What parts of her energy could go to her mom's care, and what parts needed to go to her own self-care? What of the many issues could actually be her mom's decisions and her mom's journey?

What about Beau's message to *"just feed her"*? Angela said it was ironic that the message was to "feed" her mom because her mom's occupation for many years was of all things, a nutritionist. Maybe there were deeper issues going on and maybe they were indeed important parts of her mom's journey that were coming up for her mom to deal with.

Overall, it was quite a healing session. Angela was touched by it all. I was touched as well having had a conversation with these amazing horses, experiencing their energy, their love, their excitement and their means of confirmation.

SPIRIT SPEAKS: *Tell her to just feed her...Then you'll have energy to better feed her soul.*

SPIRIT SPOTLIGHT: Expanded Thinking

Here's the expanded thought from Beau, to take "just feed her" beyond the obvious physical meaning. Angela could feed her mom physically and then have more energy so that in other ways she could feed her mom's soul, support her spirit, and be a witness to the pain and hard times without having to solve all the problems or find all the answers. She could feed her soul by just sitting with her for quality moments. She could down-size all the effort of everything else and just focus on the feeding. Well done, beloved horse.

Isn't it something that the best way Spirit could minister to Angela was through the special love and bond of her horses? It was the perfect format for Angela, the best presentation of Spirit that she could hear. Spirit knew that Angela would feel safe with the horse energy, and that being in that safe space would allow her to better hear with her heart wide open, guidance that on many levels would help her survive the challenges.

There is a beautiful lesson here that Spirit comes in unique ways, individualized for the receiver. Spirit will never barge into our life and demand to be acknowledged or accepted, but will in contrast give messages of love, support, and wisdom in a personalized, safe, and comfortable way.

The message for Angela about letting other people have their own journey has come through many times and for all types of relationships: husband and wife, parent and child, business associate with colleague, and friend to friend. Thinking about it, if you were to look at the difficult times and issues in your personal relationships, would any of them be about trying to cast judgment on or control someone else's journey? To control or manage their behavior or their decisions? Control an outcome? Is it working?

Can you imagine what it might feel like to let it go? Let them have their consequences, and let the outcomes be about their choices? Unclench our fists?? When I think about letting go of control, I feel like flying, don't you?

A client came in for Reiki who felt unhinged about how to go on even one more day with her partner of thirty three years in a relationship that was taking the life out of her. Like Angela, all the care-giving was too much. After talking some about it, the opportunity emerged to consider the very same questions as Angela had about the trappings of managing someone else's life, feeling a need to manage someone else's behaviors and decisions because of the meshed identify and care-taking that made it seem impossible to separate from them.

Spirit offered my desperate client this plan: "You will know in 21 days what to do." That was a crazy answer but with a few more details it made sense, in fact it was perfect. For starters, it gave her hope that a change was in sight while giving her time to think it all through. Then, Spirit clarified with details what to do during those 21 days.

During 21 Days of Guidance:

• Work to be grounded. Plant your feet everyday while you breathe it in.

• Find your tool for connecting with your inner, spiritual self whether it is tai chi, yoga, meditation, or journaling.

- Release your partner, your job, or situation to their/the Highest Good.

- Say out loud, "I release this".   Act it out as if cutting the cords.

- Ask and watch for signs and confirmations.

- Review your life's purpose. Define it, embrace it. What lights you up? What puts the light out?

- Choose what and who you will allow in your life going forward.
- Rest from your labor of care-taking. Rest from doing whatever it takes to hold things together at least once a day, in some way.

Any one of these steps could be difficult, so actually scheduling each one may make it easier, and the commitment to it more assured. Schedule in your alone time, quiet time, grow time, and rest time right along with everything else.

When you feel weary, take time to rest.
Retreat from your work and efforts.
Retreat to restore.
Don't worry that you are somehow not doing your job.
Rest is not a retreat from your purpose.

We are celebrating in all dimensions that you are giving us permission to be incarnate with you even as you rest
and because you can rest. In so doing, you could find the masterpiece that is you.

For now, REST is your purpose.
From this comes the harvest you will take with you.

Hunting For Answers, Counselor
Ultimately, the spirit in nature is the Source.

<u>Session Notes:</u>

I am writing these session notes because the messages from Spirit are best shared intact. I hope in the reading of them you will feel your own resonance and affirmations that Spirit comes to us in ways that mean the most with messages that answer our every question.

It will be helpful for understanding Janelle's story to know that she is a successful family counselor known for personal strength and depth of character. Janelle came in for an intuitive Reiki session wanting guidance about four things: moving forward in her profession, help understanding her lack of energy, and guidance on how she could best manage her personality snag which she described as "having difficulty with authority." She said that trait was not helpful right now as she is dealing with lawyers and judges for a legal appeal issue, which she wonders what the outcome will be. Most of all she wanted to know who her guides are.

I started by asking her the identity of God she most connects to and she replied, "I find nature most fulfilling." Hearing that, it was not surprising that the first spirit guide to step forward was Wolf who stated right away that he was Janelle's animal totem. Wolf delighted in pointing out how the attributes of wolf match Janelle's attributes of courage and strength, and how Wolf loves his clan yet is comfortable and confident as a loner just like Janelle is in her human relationships.

Wolf said, *"My Hunting skills are needed for Janelle because of their usefulness as "attentiveness" and the hunting she does as a family therapist, hunting for causes and solutions of the problems for her people. Tell Janelle to watch for signs of Wolf and she will know me as her spirit helper and guide."*

I told Janelle about Wolf's presence and Janelle was delighted. She had expected Wolf was her guide as she already had previous signs. It all resonated, and she was now going to be even more alert to signs as Wolf has suggested.

There was more to come in today's session so we continued. As I was reflecting on the Wolf connection, another guide stepped in to reveal that Janelle was a Native American Chief in another life who was named, of all names, Wolf Chief. I had never heard the name so I was interested in checking later if that was a name recorded in history. (Looked it up—it is.)

Wolf Chief spoke to Janelle saying:

It is in your DNA to know leadership skills, to love nature, and also to have conflict with authority. This comes from your role as Chief. When you were a leader, you had disagreements with other council members, and as history would reveal, you were correct in your intuitions and strategies to fight for the protection of your clans, but because you needed to submit to the majority of the council, your advice was not taken and severe consequences followed. Equally, the white man authority figures betrayed you bringing huge pain and sorrow for you and your people. It is understandable that authority figures do not sit well with you.

As a chief, you weren't able to be as much of a listener as you wished because you had to be a planner, decision maker, fighter, and stand alone as a leader with wolf courage and strength to lead your perishing clan. It became a karma wish for you to live another life in which you could above all else be a listener. It is in your DNA.

Now you have been a listener in this life. Your karma has been fulfilled so you may move on if you wish. Retire from so much listening and engage in teaching if you wish. Consider a treatment style change in your work to include more teaching.

Because there is a shift in planet consciousness, your profession must also shift its working plan. Listening is not to be forgotten, but there can be a greater emphasis on more teaching. After the minimum of listening, one will realize that the more effective healing process could be in teaching about the 'letting go' of past events and trauma.

Yes, listen to the stories, and you will know and recognize each story as familiar in human history. But then move on quickly from the telling and listening to the teaching. Move from people re-telling their story to them letting their story go; releasing the pain and sorrow by acknowledging and accepting, then saying goodbye. Look at the past, own the story, thank anyone involved for their help in co-creating the event so you could learn from it, then let it go as emotions and memories that are no longer helpful.

Be with your client, walk them through a process of putting the memory in a sacred box, lifting that box with gratitude to a Higher Power for transmuting (changing) the energy of it to the energy of love. If that act needs to be repeated, that's all right as there are many cells in their body that hold the memory. Each cell needs its chance to let go and re-fill with love and light.

About your lack of energy, while you are with your clients, to prevent your own empathic burn out, develop an empathy that is more of a sacred compassion. This compassion has a boundary that reminds you there is no need to go into depths of empathy that rob you of energy because you know that in the end, every event and happening in our lives is for the purpose of growth and learning. You know that when it's all said and done, every tragedy has a silver lining, every occurrence has been planned, and all is just as it is meant to be.

The Spirit messages could not have been more succinct. Amazing. As I continued the Reiki treatment, I could see in my mind's eye a large, beautiful eye which appeared as the eye of a dolphin; then it morphed into the eye of a whale. Then I could see the eye of a wolf, a hawk and crow. Then there were several eyes like a collage from several different animals.

I asked what the meaning was, and Spirit said for Janelle, *"These wonderful animals and spirit guides are already watching over you. Connect with them. Build a Spirit Team to help you in your work and your life. Receive. Let that be your word for the day.*

As you invite your animal totems to be on your team, receive their gifts of love, wisdom, and guidance. Ultimately, the Spirit in nature is the Source of All That Is. The spirit of your ancestors and the spirit of these amazing creatures who are watching over you is the Source of all that is. Consider letting the Source be part of your team."

As the session was coming to a close, I remembered that Janelle asked a question about the legal appeal issue. So I asked, "What will be the outcome of the appeal?"

Spirit said: *"This situation is symbolic of what we have been saying about letting go. The appeal will be more quickly resolved when you are able to let go of the outcome. Let go of your presumed responsibility to make something happen, or your desire to control what happens. Let go of your wish for this to be the means of financial preservation that you need and deserve.*

Instead let the universe be in charge of what you cannot really control anyway. Let go of the outcomes in your practice, in your relationships, in the appeal, and in your desires. It is fine to express your desires, write them and say them out loud as your wishes and prayers, and let them be there as part of your energy field. Then release all concerns about the outcomes.

You will attract more and manifest more as you let your desires be there in your heart without trying to make them happen or control how and when they appear. As you let go of the outcome, you will live from a place of alignment with your soul's true nature. This is a more assured place of attraction and manifestation.

Then when the outcome reveals itself, you again have choices about how you will respond. Imagine the outcome to be the rock, something you can't change. For example in the Appeal, see the outcome as a rock and then choose: will you stand on top of it and regardless of what it is, will you be on top saying thank you and I accept? Or will you let yourself be under it, weighed down, perhaps even smashed and overcome by the weight of it?

There is no need to be distracted by what others may choose for their life. They have their own journey to live. When their choices intersect with yours, when they disagree and object, whether it appears to be a good thing or not a good thing, you will always be loved and cherished by the Universe. Count on that.

It is a universal truth that you will always be taken care of as you live the life that you are meant to live. No mere human being and no set of circumstances can take that from you. In the worst case scenario, physical "things" can be taken, a physical life can be taken, but never the essence of you which is your soul. Your soul is protected, loved, guided, and cherished for now and for always. And so it is."

SPIRIT SPEAKS: *You will always be taken care of.*

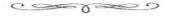

SPIRIT SPOTLIGHT: Sacred Empathy

Anyone serving in the role as a healer or lightworker would do well to meditate on sacred empathy. People in this category of service whether your profession is a counselor, nurse, Reiki practitioner, teacher, doctor, therapist, or whether you live a life of service and giving as a volunteer or simply a citizen, you are naturally empathetic. You are prone to take on more than is helpful for your own state of well-being. "Sacred Empathy" helps to balance that.

Having empathy is descriptive of a person in service, having sacred empathy is vital to well-being.

Sacred empathy, or sacred compassion as Wolf says, is how to cope with sharing with the feelings of others, staying authentically sympathetic, yet not being overwhelmed by taking on those feelings. One of my first symptoms of the work of Reiki in my life was to become very sensitive to animals and particularly their demise on the highways. Post Reiki, I had a deeper relationship with all beings, consequently, I could barely stomach seeing the deaths on the road because my empathetic response was so magnified. I was equally more horrified by humanity's inhumanity toward all of the animal kingdom.

I asked Spirit how I could possibly walk the Reiki road and survive feeling the pain of my own heartbreak from seeing them abused or hurt. This is what Spirit said:

The hardest part is the "down" side of empathy, which in contrast to depth of love and compassion is depth of pain, separation, loss, trauma, and injustice. To protect your heart, strive for Sacred Compassion which is a sacred and holy empathy that KNOWS about the truths of divinity which in turn will create a sacred boundary to protect you from going too deep with the shared pain of empathy.

A Sacred Compassion knows that while there is pain, there is also the blessing of Divine Timing, the presence of Spirit Teams and Holy Helpers, and there is Sacred Healing. There is Divine Purpose, a consecrated individual journey, and the best ending ever which is the equalizer for all living beings. That takes the edge off the hurt and pain of death, suffering, and injury felt deeply by the empath.

The application of sacred empathy is wonderfully described by Spirit in the message that we received for my client about her son. She and her husband are parents of an adult child immersed in the consequences of a Bi-Polar diagnosis. For this young man, his challenges led him far beyond a typical life style. He went from place to place, situation to degenerating situation, from cartels in Mexico to homeless solitude on the streets of city after city. As a parent, what more can you possibly do after your effort upon effort to help is not enough?

When every effort to rescue and every investment to re-start is at best, short lived and more often rejected? Spirit said:

His challenges, temptations, and choices have in their accumulation limited his perception on the front lines. His life has been full of a growing number of experiences but not a growing in depth or awakening. He has chosen limitation in this lifetime around and has built up a body of experiences but has not been able to go beyond the experiences to comprehend their meaning and to interact with their value for moving beyond the physical to the higher calling of meaning and purpose. That will come but perhaps not until another lifetime.

He has interacted with life in a way that many of us have not chosen, and that interaction has not led him to an alignment with Love as we know it. Love for the truth of life in both the physical and non-physical dimensions, although not seen and comprehended in this lifetime for him, will be available for the perceiving in lifetimes yet to come.

We may be tempted to anguish over the lost potential of this life or worry that our part was not played out well or that we should have done more. There is no need to anguish or worry or judge this life on the basis of the human perception of missed opportunity. The resistance, filters, screens, and constraints both seen and unseen will lead him through the experiences he has to where he can and will move forward at his own pace and choosing. That will in time manifest as a more positive approach in a different lifetime.

In our Service, we want to be "Fishers of Men" and to "save" them and pull them onto shore. But sometimes we need not cast the line again and again or put out a net of safety time after time. It is fine to allow the fish to grow as he chooses. It is not wasted time or a wasted life for any soul as there still is eternity to continue the journey. That is the perception of sacred empathy. Let sacred empathy give you relief and hope as you continue your life of offering much love and support to your fellow travelers.

Sacred Compassion. Live and work from there.
The work is cultivating a place where we can
state the positive and allow it to lead our thinking
to a higher place where we can see every outcome
as good in its own evolved way.

It's Just Not Right
Everyone will have their own complicated reasons.

Injustice is the theme of countless books and movies because we can all relate. It happens every day and touches all of humanity. Life either grinds to a halt from the repercussions of it, or life explodes within from the feelings experienced from an outrageous unjustness. When it comes to injustice, nothing gets up my hackles more than when it's an animal or a child on the receiving end of abusive adults disgracefully revealing their self-centeredness or spinning the truth to cover up their own behaviors or to salvage their own reputation.

Such was the case for fourteen-year-old Jesse. I got an email from his grandmother asking me to send distance Reiki to the whole family.

Jesse's grandmother explained what was going on. The story goes that Jesse was in the cafeteria for lunch where he started throwing his water bottle around. Nobody knows what started it, but he didn't stop when he was told to. Security was called, and they took him to the principal's office. He reacted with profanity at first, but then he calmed down. The administration suspended him, and held him in the office until dismissal.

As he was walking to the bus, two security guards from the high school pursued him closely, and one was heard to say, "So this is your first run-in with the law, but it won't be your last." Jesse turned around with a spit at the guard who then slammed him against the bus followed by a dead lock while the other officer came up from behind and knocked his feet out from under him. Five sheriff cars showed up, and they hog tied him with zip ties on his feet and hands behind his back. Quite the event.

When later questioned by an attorney, the guards could not remember the real sequence of events, and Jesse was charged with assault. Without defending either side, we can still ask, "What really happened?" And we can ask, "What happens to truth? Where does it go?" Injustice occurs all too often and evokes deep questions of relevance like, "Why can't people tell the truth? Why can't the truth save the day? Why do bad things happen to good people? Does God even care? Does prayer even work?"

Reflect on what Spirit said as it relates to any injustice:

Here is a situation of great concern. Yes, all prayers are heard. Prayer can surround those prayed for with love and comfort that softens and contains the emotions but also warms the ice from the rejection, harm, and cruelty. Every prayer, thought, and tear collects and comforts with great effect. It may not always be seen but it is our word that it is always helpful. Especially when you feel helpless, you can always count on the truths of the Universe such as the power of the intentional vibrations of love which is prayer.

Truth is fluid on the earth plane and can be difficult to clarify when people declare their free will and determine that their stories and reputations are more important than anyone else's, that their justifications are more valid. The heart doesn't lie so the real truth will always be known from the heart.

In the human experience, touching the heart, opening the heart, and sharing from the heart are difficult so you may never HEAR the truth without the shadowing of a varying degree of perspectives. Hear this truth from us that our beloved Jesse is worthy of sitting with Jesus, standing in the circle of Archangels, and walking in the path of golden Light surrounded by the love and compassion of many.

You have come to a situation that many face, including our own Jesus, where there was blatant injustice, where the accused are innocent, where the truth is hidden, and where the judgments are without cause and the punishments beyond comprehension. The contrasts between love and fear, good and evil are heightened by the evidence of lying and pride.

What is the path to take in the presence of injustice?

1. *Walk by faith that no matter what humanity does, God and Beings of Light have ultimate power over guidance for eternal consequences. What may appear to be endless misery will in perfect timing present with perfect relief because ultimately we are spirit and will connect with the Spirit that is above all else for guidance, protection, and blessing.*

2. *Practice using the Gifts of Prayer, Love, Family, and Friends. Lean on, indulge in, and partake in Love and Light from the resources available and from love around you.*

3. *Allow revenge to be out of your hands. Your wishes to fight back and get even will be heightened in the light of injustice and as that happens, respect your feelings as honest and understandable. But then allow them to be gifted to the forces for Good; allow the energy and power of those feelings to become forces for positivity. How? Gather them in the palms of your hands to be lifted as sacrifices to be burned, offerings of the ultimate trust that from bad can come good, and from fear can come love, and from injustice can come change.*

4. *Feel free to disengage from any of the players of the situation for the rest of your life if need be. You will see evidence of people being badly disconnected from their higher self, shockingly willing to cover up the truth, and disappointingly turning their*

back on the important matters of eternal value. You will not want to be around them which is fine. Let them go.

5. It could be helpful to treasure in your heart that not everyone is living from their place of truth at every juncture in their life, but everyone can be on their own journey as you allow them to be freed from your condemnation during that journey. That will free YOU, at any point in your life, from your own condemnation of yourself. This is what allows for the fullness of Love. Ultimately we are all here to learn and grow, and ultimately we are all worthy of compassion. Ultimately the Spirit of the Universe is without condemnation and judgment. That's called unconditional love.

6. There will come a time when understanding will open space for forgiveness and healing.

The truth is clear that behaviors in this situation were poorly chosen and injustice occurred. The series of events was unfortunate and the consequences will be unfortunate as well. Everyone will have their own perspectives, their own complicated reasons for what they admit to or don't admit to, and everyone will have their own consciences to deal with for eternity. May we all choose to remember who we are, look bravely at who we want to be, and make choices based on the Universal Truths of Light and Love. And so it is.

SPIRIT SPEAKS: *Ultimately we are spirit and will connect with the Spirit that is above all else.*

SPIRIT SPOTLIGHT: The Angst Of It

The truth does matter, but in cases like these, the truth may never be brought to Light. Sadly, it may only reside in our heart. Justice is not always served in human courts, literally and figuratively. Rather than focus on lies and deceit, with effort we can choose to focus on what will lead to healing. When do we call upon our legion of Angels to fight the battle to bring Light to the truth through judicial process? Or when do we fight the battle with the power of the sacrifice of love for acceptance and healing? That is the challenge.

When you think about it, what a surprising gift we have with Free Will and that tiny but powerful space between an event and our response to it. In that space we get to decide how we are going to respond, from a place of fear or a place of love. If our response came flying out of our mouth before we remembered that we had a choice, then no worries, you will get another chance as life moves along. We can decide how we want to live, and we can practice making those choices every day so it becomes more likely to occur more naturally and on our first impulse.

What about the angst of it? We get to use our angst to make a difference where things need to change, to refine justice, to love when we can, and to be who we want to be. We get a chance to decide and practice trusting our Source.

Have you ever witnessed humanity's inhumanity to humans? Or animals? I can barely tolerate it. I asked my friend, Toby, one day how he could live through it. Toby is a handsome and proud percheron horse who has witnessed firsthand cruel and brutal treatment. Through the wonders of telepathy and animal communication, Toby said:

We are individuals and we are a collective. It helps us to trust you even more when we realize that you hear and see us as a kingdom, part of the planet, and ultimately one with every living thing. Unconditional love is our nature. That nature can be damaged by trauma and abuse.

You might say it is unforgivable how some humans treat animals. We say any heart can be forgiven for choices that were made from a place of disconnect with the soul.

When you witness injustice, help when you can. Advocate and speak up for justice and change. Pray and send positive healing thoughts. Seek to understand and choose higher thoughts of acceptance and forgiveness. Give love and be a witness. Embrace Sacred compassion.

Any heart can be forgiven for choices that were made from a place of disconnect with the soul.

Keeper of Wisdom
Tell her to laugh harder, dance wilder, and tell more jokes!

As always before giving a Reiki treatment, I invited energies of love and healing to join us. This treatment was for Danielle so I stated that our intention was for the time and energy to be given to her for her highest healing and highest good. A wonderful group energy came forward saying, *"Tell Danielle how much we love her and we are so proud of her."*

It was such a fun, lively spirit group full of spit and fire as they say. I told them I'd be happy to give Danielle a message, could I tell her who it was from? *"I'm her grandmother. We are her family. We are all so proud of her. Look at what she does and who she has become."*

I was happy to meet them and asked, "What could I tell Danielle about you that would confirm who you are?" I could hear an "L" but couldn't quite get the full name. So Spirit said, *"She'll know me. I'm the one that she looks like. Tell her we love her. Oh, and tell her to laugh more. Tell her to laugh harder, dance wilder, and tell more jokes!"*

I asked Danielle if she had a grandmother who has passed and she said, "Yes I do. Her name is Lucy, and I look just like her." We talked about a few more happy things.

I would have loved to talk more with this vivacious and loving soul and family group, but I could feel the energy shift to the head of the Reiki table. The energy coming in there felt huge and magnificent. I intuitively knew it was a Spirit Guide. I was experiencing the presence of Love and Power. The colors all around us were waves of celestial blues and shimmers of Light. I took a few moments to take it all in, then

I asked who was with us, did they have a name. The Spirit said, *I am William, the Keeper of Wisdom.*

We do not need names. Our identity is in Who We Are. However, when you ask, we are happy to bring names forward that you, who are on the earth plane, can relate to and would feel comfortable in using. I was called Black Hawk by Geronimo. I appeared to him as a black hawk. I bring this up because Danielle saw me in that life. She saw me as a Black Hawk and knew that I was a Spirit of Great Wisdom.

Her life was very short that time around as her lessons were experienced early on. She lived only as a child and came back to Spirit following a water event.

In my mind's eye I saw a picture of a young child being pulled under by a rapidly flowing river. I could feel the horror of it. Then I could see this man in a posture of sorrow and despondency. I asked and was told it was Geronimo, broken by the loss of the child and broken by the tragedy of also losing his land, his nation, and the inheritance of his people. I could feel the intensity and passion of his seeking the wisdom of Black Hawk.

I was Black Hawk to Geronimo. He cried tears as he pleaded for our wisdom. He was so baffled by the white man's nation and what they were doing to his nation. It was impossible to understand the white man's need to destroy and plunder, to dominate and desecrate the earth; to assault the animal kingdom, to annihilate his tribe and their land.

I bring this story to light as a pure example of contrast. It was the lovers of nature versus the lovers of power, the seekers of Spirit versus the seekers of supremacy. In the light of such contrast then and contrast in any generation, what is there to do but seek Wisdom. I am with Geronimo, I am with Danielle and I am with many souls as the Keeper of Wisdom.

Touched by the vision and the story, I had to sit down. I could feel and see what it might have been like. I wanted to tell all nations and all how sad I felt about the unjust and deeply grieving times that permeate our history.

I asked Black Hawk, "There are so many times we need wisdom. How do we receive Wisdom? How does it work? Sometimes we ask for help and we don't hear anything. Or we hear something and question if we really did. Did we make it up? Or sometimes we say what we think we heard, and it doesn't seem all that wise. Do you know what I mean?"

Every intentional asking, every intentional seeking of connection to Spirit is like collecting the resources. You can put them in your back pocket. Every intentional action of seeking will give you a bit of wisdom that you can collect. That collection will be there when you need it. Keep asking, keep seeking connection, and keep collecting your wisdom.

I asked, "What could be said that would be a confirmation for Danielle that you are indeed a Guide who she can trust and learn to know?"

"Ask her what Gift of the Spirit she is seeking. Tell her I am holding the space of Wisdom for her which will lead her to understanding and compassion which is what she is seeking. Call on me. And so it is."

It touched my heart and felt like a reassuring Truth worth repeating: "I am holding the space of Wisdom for her." So personal, so available. Later in the Reiki treatment, I asked Danielle the questions Black Hawk said to ask, "What Gift of the Spirit are you seeking?" She answered, "Compassion." Just what Black Hawk had said.

What better way to grow our compassion than by living in the Light of Wisdom. Wisdom with its understanding takes us to a place of empathy, forgiveness, and compassion. Divine Wisdom reveals to us the ultimate truth that we are ALL ONE. Standing in the place of Oneness, we *suffer* the hurt when another hurts, we *celebrate* joy when another feels joy, and we *know* that giving to any living thing is giving to our self. In the Light of Wisdom, we comprehend that we are all living an intentional journey, that we have agreed to be together in the journey, and hallelujah we have a purpose that links us to each other.

While intentional in the seeking of wisdom, the living of it manifests Love and Light filling our heart until it flows as compassion. It does so not only naturally but with enthusiasm! Now that's compassion.

SPIRIT SPEAKS: *Keep asking, keep seeking connection, and keep collecting your wisdom.*

❦

SPIRIT SPOTLIGHT: Keeper of Reiki Wisdom

Keeper of Wisdom for Reiki

A speaker, teacher, master, international mentor and "Keeper of Wisdom" for Reiki is William Rand. He has spent a lifetime researching, discovering, and sharing with incredible depth from his heart what he has learned about Reiki. I have been to several classes of his and have appreciated not only all the information and applications given in the classes but, more importantly, the energy of Reiki that he brings to the experience. He embodies an energy that heals, guides, and opens up understanding and sacred wisdom.

His passion for Reiki has led to collating an accurate history of Reiki, to gathering and inspiring research into why and how it works, and doing the work of birthing an organization and international association for the strengthening of Reiki and for protecting the purity of it called the International Center for Reiki Training, the Center for Reiki Research, and the Reiki Membership Association. He is a writer, publisher, editor, and manager of the *Reiki News Magazine* and has authored several books. He has literally gone to all ends of the planet with the Reiki messages and also to plant medallions of peace in key portals on the planet. While doing all this, with love and respect, he honors all Reiki schools and lineages.

Willam's spiritual inspirations and courage have led to creating advanced levels of Reiki as testimony to one of the basic premises that he teaches which is this: "There is always more." I have heard him say it many times and have read it in his literature. The thought is worth pondering for the benefit of applying it, for knowing that we will never rust out from boredom because there is always more to learn and experience, an infinity of more levels. We will never boast that we know it all because that just won't happen because there is always more.

The application becomes helpful when we hit a wall of limiting beliefs. When it seems too far "out there" to embrace energy work like Reiki or long distance Reiki, self-Reiki or self healing, eternal life or past lives, communication with Spirit or communication with the departed, consider this: "There is always more." There is always another step, another pilgrimage, more to embrace, more yes's to possibilities. There is always more of God to reach for, a deeper and wider expression of God to grasp, and an ever-expanding realm of the multidimensional and the multiverse to inherit as we embrace the Universal Law of One.

When I look out at the universe, there is always more. When I look at the inner workings of my body, there is always more going on in there than I can imagine. When I activate and stretch my spirituality, there is always more. When I get a grasp of who God is and my relationship with Divinity, there is always more. When I feel the satisfaction of resonance and peace, I know there is even more.

Are my beliefs limiting beliefs? Our ascended masters incarnated to better model expanded thinking. For example, Jesus came to offer a way to connect to God that was different than needing animal sacrifices or needing to go through a priest. We can ask the masters, we can ask Jesus, is there anything more you want me to know? Ask God, in light of our multidimensional world, is there anything more than what I've been taught over the years that you want me to know about who you are and what you expect from humanity?

I love that I can share more about this Native American connection that my client has. We learned more from other Reiki treatments together that brought me once again to marvel at the wonder of connections with Spirit. Without my detailing the entire back story, enjoy the messages and wisdom about past lives, unending love, and practical guidance from other visits with Danielle's guide. This is what Black Hawk said:

~There is meaning in the CD of music that you were led to bring to your Reiki treatment today, Joanne Shenandoah, "Life Blood," because there is Native American life blood within you. It is your pedigree, your ancestry, and your genetics to be of the Native American culture and its traditions. You have purposefully been blessed with the forgetting of that for the purpose of remembering anew. When you remember anew, it will be with greater depth that you revitalize your natural connection to the earth.

~The renewed connection to nature and wildlife and the wonders of natural creation will give you a tremendous sense of unconditional love. That is the essence of nature, and it will be given to you not only for yourself but as a gift that you will be giving more of to others.

~As you let go of grief, as you let go of your completed and fulfilled karma wish, and as you let go of anything that is no longer helpful, then energetic space will be created for you to receive more. That space will allow more forgiveness, compassion, and love.

~You are indeed connected with the Native American traditions especially with nature. Continue to watch for signs and totems. These are a means of communicating with you and giving you messages directly from Spirit.

~A practical activity from the Guides:
Consider for your process of letting go and renewal to have a burning ceremony. Write down the things you want to let go of on a piece of paper, then burn the paper and as the smoke rises, know that your prayers and wishes for letting go are fulfilled. Your heart and soul will in turn be filled with love, forgiveness, and compassion.

~With an incredible gentleness, the Native American chief spoke as he reached his arms out toward my client, *"This is my Shenandoah. This is my precious Shenandoah."*

As we discovered after the session, Shenandoah means "beautiful daughter of the stars." Shenandoah also means "brave." We are all brave for following our intuition, for doing what we need to do to listen to our heart and our soul. Remember the note about how my client felt led to bring the particular CD of music to the session? The composer and musician's name is Shenandoah. A coincidence?

Consider this mantra:
"I am a beautiful daughter and son of the stars."

SECTION III: PHYSICAL CHALLENGES

Address It Full On
It's about how much you can learn.

"Wasn't he just the greatest??" Everyone was buzzing. From all the times that I've seen variations of the play adaptation of *The Elephant Man*, Sid is the best ever at playing that part. How stunning the realism, effective the message, and curiously handsome the man. I overheard another audience member say, "Did you see him when he played Sweeney in *Sweeney Todd*? We didn't want to miss a single word." Acting was surely the right profession for Sid, his continuing success proved that. The standing ovations, the applause, the invitations to go on tour, and I could see in his countenance the personal satisfaction from knowing he was living his purpose.

Then came the illness. It was later that February when I was surprised to learn that Sid was unexpectedly at home in the care of his parents. He had been diagnosed with Stage Four Non-Hodgkin's Lymphoma. This cancer is in the lymphatic system and develops in cells called lymphocytes, a white blood cell that normally helps the body fight infections. Dangerously invasive, it can progress to the lymph nodes, bone marrow, spleen, thymus and digestive tract. The good news is that it is curable. At Stage Four, however, no one knew for sure. We knew that Sid would address it full on.

The prognosis was a life-changer for Sid, stopping him short in his fast track to the big stage. Cancer causes you to take a hard look at the worst and hope for the best. Part of his plan included Reiki treatments, so we set up appointments with the intention of relaxing his body to give it maximum support for healing and managing the difficult and challenging effects from the chemo and radiation.

When he came in, we talked about illness and cancer and together asked the questions: Why did Sid have to get cancer? Why at this critical time in his life? What are we to learn from it? We knew from experience that cancer is multilayered in its impact, physical, emotional, and spiritual. It is costly, complicated, and overwhelming with so many questions to answer, options to research, and issues to address. You need your own advocates and a whole team to help navigate the path. Sid had his team and was determined to get through this.

Sid's story will be short, not because Sid died. He is still alive and healthy ten years now. But short because the message from Spirit was so profound, individualized, succinct, and powerful that no more needs to be said. This one message from Spirit made all the difference in the world for Sid, how he was able to handle his situation, how fast he healed and how quickly he was able to move on to manifest the service that is his purpose in life. Here is the message:

We know you. Your life is and always has been about meaning. You've always searched for meaning in relationships, in your work, and in what you are here for. This journey with Hodgkin's Lymphoma is the best way at this time in your life to work on this goal. Getting the cancer is not about making a mistake, doing something wrong, or being a bad person. It's about what you can learn and how much you will grow in your goal which you said is to find meaning in life.

It's also a way to enhance your creativity. You are already very creative, but there is more for you. This will bring out a whole new dimension. During your lifetime you will create something magnificent. Like Noah did in the building the Ark. Well, not that big in size, but that big in magnificence. Just like Noah, you will be building it from the bottom up.

You have been worried. We understand. You have been asking yourself the question, "Will the cancer prevent you from having children?" No, it won't. You'll be fine, and your children will be fine. And you'll be the greatest dad ever.

Think on these things. Every life has meaning in many aspects. Above all else, in everything that happens and in all that is, there is meaning for the Soul. At any point in your journey when the path seems vacant of recognizable meaning, or veers off the direction you thought meaning was taking you, or brings to you traumatizing events where meaning is crushed, remember that We know you. We love you. Ask for perspective. Ask for purpose. Ask for answers. Ask for meaning. We are here.

I gave Sid his message, and I could see a look of wonder on his face. He said he was mostly astonished by the message that he will be able to have children. He asked, "How did you know I was worried about that? My biggest worry of all has been that after all this will I be able to have children?" That's the way of Spirit, to know and to answer.

For Spirit to bring that up was confirmation for Sid. It was Spirit, the Spirit who loved him and wanted him to know that this illness was about learning and growing, not punishment or retribution. It wasn't his fault or his doom and was not because he made a mistake somewhere sometime. This part of the journey was planned all in his favor. The relief from this message transformed the tragic to the a-ha. Sid was no longer weighed down by the negative, and he could radiate the positive attitude that helped him heal and be happy today.

SPIRIT SPEAKS: *Above all else, in everything that happens and in ALL THAT IS, there is meaning for the Soul.*

SPIRIT SPOTLIGHT: Accidents

I got an email from my friend and massage therapist, Robert. "A week ago I broke my wrist. Can you believe it? I'm a massage therapist! I fell in the driveway trying to move some very heavy top soil. Now I can't work for at least 8 weeks. Upsetting. I can't deal with this on top of everything else happening all at once."

Robert lives a few states away so I wasn't much practical help, but I was happy to connect with his Guides for a message of encouragement. Put your name in this story because I know the message is meant for all of us.

"Our dearest beloved -- you are such a hard worker, and giver of love and compassion. Did you ever wonder what it would feel like to rest? And receive? And allow? And take in?

We are never wanting you to feel pain and discouragement, but when something happens that puts you in a position of needing rest and recovery, we would like to ask you to let your Angels both in Spirit and on earth serve you and love you. Invite them in.

Experiment with the questions: Can you trust Us now when it appears as though your routine has been taken away? Can you trust Us now when in place of your routine is something new, different, and a place where you think you are not about to get what you think you need like a paycheck?

Experiment with visualizing this: place your resting chair on top of the highest mountain. From that higher place, lean back and watch for signs of Our love, Our leading, and Our watching over you with the heart of God, the eyes of eternity's values, and the wings of surrender.

Although it doesn't sound like a picture that makes sense, meditate on what it could really mean to be in that lounge chair nearly touching the stars of the universe knowing that you are a Child of the Creator of the universe. We love you so much. You are a Child of Light and Love. Your service is exceptional and so appreciated by the covenant of angels and ascended spirits that surround you always. You will be well soon. Take heart, beloved!"

We all know what it's like for life to be put on hold due to an accident or illness. Sometimes several things happen at once. I wonder if it takes that to get our attention. There was a period of two months in my own life when it seemed my right and dominant arm took a real beating. A bee sting on my right hand turned into cellulitis up the arm, then I got poison ivy on that hand. A week later, I landed hard on that arm when I fell off a ladder onto concrete. A month later had an axillary tumor and lymph nodes removed from you guessed it, my right arm. My body had my attention. I needed to slow down.

Spirit said to me,

Consider in your wish to ascend, that the balance of body, soul, and spirit will lead you forward. To find balance, you may need to stop in your tracks, and for the moment, just be. Could you stop in your tracks to receive? Could you let God be your arm and your brain and let that lead to your heart?

Stop the push and let your drive be more of an "allow." Give opportunity to see the magic in letting God. Here, in this place of necessary stop, take time to revive, enlighten, and receive in order to prepare for the next step. Balance yourself in order to best manifest.

May I receive the Gift of all that I need by
letting go of all that I have
To become all that I am for the purpose of shining a
Light on the Source of All That There Is.

Tina'a Animals Step Up
Family steps up, especially in times like these.

Bobbie texted to ask if I would give Reiki to her friend Tina who has Lou Gehrig's disease. Knowing that she was dying, more than anything Tina wanted to communicate with her pets. She was so worried about them. With so many questions about her future, she wondered how they were doing. I was happy to set up an appointment, send distance Reiki, or whatever was needed. I asked Bobbie to send me the names of Tina's pet and photos if possible.

In the meantime, I went to work and it turned out to be one of those days. I walked in the Center to find that water had leaked from the 2nd floor to the 1st floor and down into the basement, and in that section the whole ceiling had fallen through. What a mess. We pulled out the furniture to dry, took down the overhead lights where the water leaked through the fixtures, and we cleaned up the mess of wet sheet rock which had scattered all over.

Finished with that, I thought it would be a better day until I couldn't get the computer to connect to the internet so I couldn't print the business checks. Then I tried to complete my online checkin for my next day's flight from New York to Utah but got stopped by a glitch with the country code. These days never end. I finally got home and of course the sweet potatoes came out of the oven so hard I needed a steak knife to cut them. When does that ever happen? Could ice cream salvage this day?

Surprisingly, I got to bed at a decent hour which was a good thing because I woke up in the middle of the night. I tried but couldn't get back to sleep so I finally looked at the clock which read 2:00 AM. Wondering why I was awake so early, I realized it was the buzzing in my ears that woke me. That buzzing is my vibrational signal that someone in spirit has something to say to me telepathically. So I sat up in my bed, reached for my journal and pen, and asked, "Who wants to talk?"

We are Tina's collective of animal friends.

"Oh, hi. I thought I was going to meet you after getting your names and pictures. But this is OK. Welcome. I'm impressed that you found me in the middle of the night. So, Hi guys. I don't know your names. What shall I call you?"

Call us Tina's Furry Collective. We have things to say that we want Tina to know. We are her family, and family steps up in times like these.

Tina is very sad about what life has brought to her. It's a devastating set of circumstances. We want her to know that everything will be OK. We know that. We are used to having to live in the moment, facing uncertainties yet knowing some certainties about life. One certainty is the need to live in the moment because, well, we have very short life spans.

Every one of us, as her fur family, is here because of her extended love for us. We extend our love and hearts to her.

Each of us are looking at each other and talking to each other. Your word is "telepathically" but we would just say we share. We share, too, with Tina and what she is going through. It's a collective experience that we have. We've been through the illness process, and we've been through the death process because we've had other lives too. We have come to Tina just for this reason—to walk with her through it all.

This is what we want her to know:

- *We love you! Your life has such purpose. You have loved, and that's what the purpose is for all of us, to love. So you are a winner there. Mission accomplished.*

- *Your soul loves the Earth School experience so it will continue with its purpose to love and support your tribe and pack even when you think your body is letting you down, even when you think your Earth School life has let you down. Your soul will continue.*

- *There is no letting down. Your life, your body, and your love is not letting anyone down. In fact, it's a grand design. That understanding will come to you more and more in time. You will know that any of us as living beings are really in our essence "spirit", and that spirit moves about as a soul recognizable as the "you" that is who you are. That soul has its noble purpose, and that soul will continue fulfilling its service while you remain in your body. It will continue with that service when you transform outside of this body. Your soul, in fact, does its best work as an eternal design not always needing or wanting a body to dwell in.*

- *Don't worry about any of us! We're OK with this grand design that we are part of with you. In fact, we are honored to share these next steps with you. It'll be harder for you than it will be for us. You aren't so used to being dependent on others to care for you. We're pretty used to that. And we're pretty used to communicating from the heart. So even when your physical body seemingly lets you down, your heart will still beat with a love that we can feel and a love that has great meaning to us even when it is a mere vibration, a mere beat. That expression is enough. Maybe not what you are used to and not what you want, yet it is enough. We will always feel it, receive it, and give it back to you.*

- *We know about these things you are going through because we just know. We can patiently experience the next months with you as they bring us what they bring us. And that's because we know the big picture. We know that after we are done with this earth experience we always go right back home, the home that is the eternal place where there are lots of fields to play in, lots of sunshine to enjoy, and where there is no trauma to endure, no sadness to experience, and no enemies or fights. There are no feelings of letting anyone down or letting ourselves down. Do you know that from home we can continue with our love purpose? We keep on beating with that vibration of love and can send lots of love back to our pack who are still having an earthly experience.*

- *We are here for you. And we will help you to live in the moment. We are good at that. Did you know that living in the moment is all you need to do? And as you learn more and more about that, you will help others to appreciate their moments more, and that's a good thing. All souls can use a healthy reminder that we best serve our soul by living in the moment. There is less fear when living in the moment. We would like to lessen your fear by helping you pay attention to the moments of life.*

- *Remember always that we love you. All your two-legged human earth friends love you, too, and we don't know how you all live without fur. We will love you no matter what state of mind you are experiencing, no matter what deterioration of the physical body you may notice, and no matter what prognosis you anticipate. You would do the same for us! You would love us through it, and we will love you through it.*

- *Our advice to you? Take in each day with whatever it has to offer you. The gifts are yours. Notice what you can. Receive what you can. And don't worry about what you can or cannot give back because just being who you are is enough. Remember, even just a simple beating of your heart is enough because you are spirit, and you are love at your very core. That's the energy of life. Eternal life. And it goes on forever.*

- *We are blessed to be in your pack! It's onward and forward for all of us. How great that we can all support each other as we all have these paths that we choose for our experiences and our evolving. I bet you didn't know we knew such big words.*

Lots of kisses and hugs, Your Furry Collective

Dear Furry Collective,

Thank you, sweet collective. You are quite the pack with amazing gifts of wisdom and love. I share back to you the gift of the energy of love with all its potentials and smiles, its Light and Completeness. You do have quite the vocabulary.

Love, Sharyn

SPIRIT SPEAKS: *We best serve our soul by living in the moment.*

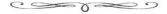

SPIRIT SPOTLIGHT: Animals Love, Teach, and Speak

They do! Much of the world has experienced the unconditional love of a pet. Many people have been impressed with animal behaviors and community living that reflect a remarkable acceptance, cooperation and communication with each other. Books and movies have been showing us what animals teach us about ourselves, about life, death, and life again. But fewer people have experienced a two-way telepathic conversation. When it happens for you, there will be no doubt that yes, animals can communicate across the species lines. To experience it for yourself, start with an animal communicator.   See what is given to you.

Reiki has been a tool for me that keeps leading me on step by step discoveries to animal communication.   At every point I hear myself saying over and over, "wow, how can that be, that's incredible, and you can't make these things up."

Reiki, with its gentle and progressive expansion, is healing me, building up my inner psychic circuits, and opening doors to what is and what can be.   Reiki is a tool that takes me to the quiet places within myself that expand with a colorful explosion of the world that is totally connected through vibration which is telepathy. With all the separation in the world, it is hard to imagine the opposite which is connection. But we are connected, not only human to human but human to animal and plant kingdoms. We connect and we can communicate.

One means of communication is the telepathic potential every living thing has which is hearing and understanding through vibration. Words, thoughts, and pictures can be felt, understood, and shared simply by sending and receiving them through energetic frequencies.

When you observe the wonders of the world, is that too much of a stretch?   When you read about advances in all sciences, medicines, and arts, when you see the biology of humanity in motion showing what our body does to perform each basic function, is it hard to understand that we create vibration? When you telescope out to the reaches of the Universe and Multiverse, is it such a leap to consider the possibility that there are other living beings with intelligence and who communicate? Even our cells display an intelligence with communication that is mind blowing.   It makes sense that the members of our Animal and Plant Kingdoms have intelligence, communicate with each other, and communicate with us.

The sure path to belief is to experience it yourself. I sincerely hope you don't dismiss the possibilities of what is happening in the world through telepathy until you try it. You may need some guidance at first, but try it for yourself.

Through science based evidence, animal communication is plausible. Experiencing the evidence first hand, it is certain. Collect your own faith builders of synchronicities, your observations, and testimonies. The best evidence of all is in your own resonance. Their voices are quiet to the ear, but loud to the heart.

May the gift of communication in its mysticism
become majestic in the places that it leads you,
to the inner seeds of your soul or to the outer
expansions of your outstretched arms and
open heart to embrace the
Universe of Infinity.

Am I The Pain In My Neck?
What are you not being flexible about?

"Mr. Johnson, I'm sorry to tell you that the arthritis in your neck is causing severe inflammation. That's what is giving you the pain, and that's why you can't move your neck. The breathing problem will get worse before it gets better. We have done all that we know to do. Your extended use of tobacco over so many years has caused permanent damage in your lungs and…" the doctor's voice faded as all Zach could focus on now was the anger and helplessness he felt at the prospect of the news.

I had scheduled a full day giving Reiki treatments even though it was Christmas Eve. I intended to finish my day a little early. After all, it was a holiday. I happened to be between clients at the moment and was in a place where I could answer my ringing cell phone. I heard a man on the other end say, "This is Zach. Is there any chance I can get Reiki today? I am in a lot of pain." I didn't know who Zach was or how he got my number, but I heard myself saying, "I'm totally booked, but I'll push my schedule out if you can come in by 4:00."

He knew his business meeting that day would have to end in time for him to make it. Fortunately, it did, and as he came through the door, Zach asked, "Could I have both massage and Reiki?" I tag- teamed with the massage therapist still at the office, and we got started.

Consulting with Zach, he told us his story and explained that he was suffering from several issues. He could not move his neck without excruciating pain, could barely breathe, and felt scared about his heart problems. He explained that he was here because he wanted to "build up his life vitality and energy and heal himself." I sensed that this husky, masculine Native American was a spiritual and determined man on a healing journey.

I prepared the room for the two-hour back-to-back massage and Reiki. It had been a busy day in the office. For the entire previous seven hours of the day, the typical spa music had been shuffling on the iPod, and at this point, I was content to let the shuffle continue. Wouldn't you know it, the minute he came in the room for the treatment, a Native American song came on. I noticed it because it was perfect for the atmosphere of healing and strengthening that Zach could relate to. I didn't know this was about to happen, but the drumming and Native American flute played solid for the next two hours. More on that later.

After his massage, Zach stayed on the massage table, and I came in to give him Reiki. Our treatment goal was to balance Zach's chakras and life energy knowing that the relaxing and balancing would put his body in an optimal place to heal itself. As always, I asked for and invited the presence of help from Ascended Masters, Guides, and Spirit Healers.

A Reiki energy scan confirmed what Zach had said about his medical issues with nearly all the chakras showing blocked energy centers. I double checked with a pendulum, and there was a strong indication that he was "giving out more than he is taking in," which can mean literally giving out more time, more love, more money, more energy, and more resources than he allowed to come back in to his life to re-fill the reservoir. "Giving out" can also mean talking more than listening, literally giving out more words than you are taking in. That resulting imbalance and depletion can hinder healing and the flow of energy and strength, and I was confident Reiki would help.

I appreciated feeling the familiar heat and pulsing of the Reiki energy and knew that healing was taking place. I began working on the neck points when I clearly heard Spirit verbalize a question, *"Ask him what he is not being flexible about."* It didn't feel like a character judgment but merely a question as if to recommend some serious thinking. The Guide spoke again, "Ask him that."

Before saying anything to Zach, I wanted to make sure who I was hearing so I asked who the Spirit was.

"I am Zach's Guide." I could see in my mind's eye that he was a leader and Chief in full headdress. His presence was truly impressive! He could have been intimidating, but his energy was so gracious and loving that I felt totally at peace. Humbled, I welcomed him and expressed gratitude that he was with us.

The Guide continued:

Zach is a man of great influence and leadership. Yes, this current medical journey is part of his leadership story. These difficult physical issues will teach, guide, and help him lead others. For now, ask him what he is not being flexible about.

We understand that it can be very difficult to be flexible. Our standards of culture, family, government, and laws can make it seem impossible to bend the rules or the boundaries. Perhaps there is a misguided tenacity, misinformation, or simply a lack of clarity about an issue so we don't allow movement or change.

However, being inflexible for whatever the reason limits what you see around you, prevents you from seeing all sides, and inhibits you from adapting a good plan and experiencing success. Zach, just like what your pain in the neck is causing, you are not rotating your vision, not seeing all sides of the story, and it's stopping you from moving forward.

Tell that to Zach. Tell him, 'Your severe neck pain will resolve when you take a look at what you are not being flexible about. Follow my guidance.

Ready to share with Zach what I heard, I started by asking him, "Do you believe in Guides?" He seemed surprised at first but said, "Yes, I certainly do believe in guidance from our ancestors."

I told him about his Guide and the message he gave. Zach replied, "That makes a lot of sense to me. I want to think about that." He closed his eyes and the moments of stillness that followed felt sacred with a presence of sanctified energy.

In the quietness, I noticed the music once again, and the vocal on the song was a Native American voice speaking in a native tongue. It was serene and powerful. I didn't understand the words until the vocalist next translated the message into English: "We are One with nature, One with God and One with Divinity." I was touched by the soulful reminder of the Universal Truth of Oneness and the divine decree that we love one another.

As the song track ended, I quietly asked Zach how he was doing. He opened his eyes and said, "I got the answer. I got the answer!" I saw a brightened countenance, an expression of peacefulness, and a look of relief on his face. I knew he was moving forward in his healing journey.

Was Zach's behavior causing his pain in his neck? Recognition about lessons from our physical pain served in this case to inspire change.

SPIRIT SPEAKS: *"Your severe neck pain will resolve when you take a look at what you are not being flexible about."*

⚬⚬⚬

SPIRIT SPOTLIGHT: Behind the Physical Challenges

There may be a direct connection between physical pain and emotional or spiritual pain. If that resonates with you, be gentle with yourself and others as we all look for the courage to discover truth behind our illness and take whatever action is needed to change and to heal. What a gracious gift from Spirit when the connection is made clear.

In this case, the physical issues brought up good questions for Zach. What was he not being flexible about? On the job, at home, in relationships, in the rules of order, about a stand, in the clan? And why?

There can be a strength and a gentleness in flexibility especially when allowing others to live their journey. After all, it is their journey. That is where others will find their own strength, by connecting to their own process and purpose. Blessed are the merciful to give people space and to hold them and their space gently and reverently as we all find our way. This is the power of the Universal Law of Oneness, the application of the truth that we are all One, all here on a journey sharing space and benevolence.

Two important points: First, we can always ask for guidance in finding truth behind our physical challenges. I find it fascinating that we can ask our God, our spiritual Guides, and we can ask our own body, "What is it that I can learn from this?" Consider asking your head, for example, why is it aching? When we discover a connection and hear the message, it can be life-changing.

Secondly, the Spirit message I hear most often about physical illness is that health issues and pain are *never* about punishment. Whether a sliver, a migraine, cancer, or a litany of problems, health issues are not a result of or about the need for discipline, chastisement, or retribution.

In the direct words of Spirit about another one of my clients: *There are many reasons for his health issues but none are about a judgment on his life and not about breaking down his ego. He has done nothing wrong, and this is not about karma. It is easy for humans to look at themselves and ask what have we done to deserve this.*

This client had quite a long list of problems, among them bursitis, bilateral knee pain, chronic pain syndrome, lumbar-sacral spondylosis without myelopathy, spinal stenosis, mixed hyperlipidemia, chronic diarrhea, bilateral shoulder dislocation, rotator cuff tear, esophageal reflux, anxiety disorder, impotence, essential hypertension, internal hemorrhoids, plantar fasciitis, colitis, and eight concussion accidents. Unbelievable but true.

I asked Spirit, "What could be the positive benefits of so many health issues?" Spirit replied:

These are Positive Benefits of health issues:
* *They give the impetus for closer connection with family, one's spiritual side, and God.*
* *It's a reminder to ask, "What is most important to give time and effort to?"*
* *We get to look and learn about the body and see the marvels of its creation.*
* *Illness inspires appreciation for the miracle and Source of the body and health.*
* *It's a reminder about the fragility of the body and life, therefore the value of each day.*
* *It's a prompting to be PRESENT as you live; there may be no tomorrow.*
* *Illness has a cost and is thus a reminder that money is a facilitator not the goal of life.*
* *It reminds us that family is a partnership, illness is not a burden to carry alone.*
* *It remind us that we have choices about our health, life style, diet, work, and play.*

Tell our Beloved that this is not the end of his life, unless he wants it to be. Otherwise, it's the beginning of the next phase and cycle. Call it "Life After Diagnosis" where each day matters and each moment is expanded to absorb life to the fullest. Time must turn around from a "count-down to the end" to become a measure of special moments upon special moments; a gift of life rather than a march to death.

I asked, "How can I help him? Is there anything I can do?"

It's hard for him to let go of the world he has come to know. His body is a picture of chaos as every body element is trying to do its part to bring balance and healing. Every organ is working overtime; the tissues are drowning in the constant effort. It's what it might be like if one was flying too high and too fast to land. But he really wants to land. When he tries to land he pulls up because it's scary.

How may you help? Suggest he fly back around and try again with some pre-paving first, pre-paving meaning work that can be done before the next treatment. For starters, his body is so full of pharmaceuticals they are making him sick. As he surrenders to their presence and power, he can organize and conduct a gradual minimization or withdrawal. That is step one.

Next, pre-pave with continuing efforts of prayer and "long distance Reiki" seeing him well and asking for the universal Reiki energy to give him healing. Pre-paving means focusing intentions on seeing him healthy, seeing him receptive to energy help, and seeing him finding relief in the promise and hope that he will indeed feel better in the days to come.

Re-affirm his ego and his value. When we lose our health, we often lose our sense of worth.

It is in acceptance that you find the soothing.
Not in miraculous cures that take pain away, but
in the acceptance of the sacred
which has reasons of its own.

Rock Bottom
This, by the way, distracts one's thinking from
the painful reasons for dying to
the healing reasons for living.

You think hitting rock bottom will be the thing to turn circumstances around until you hit rock bottom 20 times, and find it's still not the thing.

He said it wasn't his fault. Someone spiked his drink, then stole his car. So he borrowed another, then crashed and totaled it on the way home. He was injured in the wreck but survived. He had to serve jail time and pay fines for four citations. That led to the divorce. Then he lost his job and had to sell his house. Enough?

That was just one small part of Murph's story, a client's son addicted to both alcohol and street drugs. It seemed like a lifetime for these parents still hoping that their son would hit that final rock bottom that will cause him to change his life. In response to "What can we do for Murph?" Spirit's message offers a practical technique for breaking the cycles of addiction.

Spirit, how can we help Murph? What is your advice for helping anyone addicted to drugs, and their life collapsing around them? How can we as parents, spouses, brothers & sisters, and friends help addicts?

My dear humans, it is with great difficulty that souls navigate life with its mazes and lessons especially while under the influence of mind-altering substances. While it may appear at first that these substances are of benefit, the benefit is temporary, and the not-so-beneficial consequences are not.

The wisdom for how to help someone consists of varying options, and we suggest putting effort into each. Your love for the person with addiction is a driving force that can help them beyond measure on their healing path. Every single soul is a vital force in the Universe. Know that we, too, wish to see Murph able to live his earth experience from a place of joy and well-being rather than the disconcerting place of addiction.

Once a soul is addicted to the attachment of the influencing and altering effects of drugs of any form, disengagement from that addiction becomes a multidimensional path of healing that includes recovery on complex levels. It is molecular, chemical, physical, emotional, mental, and spiritual. Know that although complex, it is indeed possible and well worth the journey for the soul who wishes to evolve for their Highest Good.

To start, suggest to Murph, in his most lucid moment possible, to create a Bucket List. The act of writing it can give him a sense of purpose even though he believes his life isn't worth anything. No matter what state of mind he may be in at any moment, denial has its limits when the "writing is on the wall" so to speak. When it is written, dated, signed, and posted somewhere, he could recognize that there are lucid moments and there are not so lucid moments, undeniably. In clear times, there is meaning to life and goals to reach for.

In the lucid moments, the creation of a Bucket List gives value on many levels. It brings one to the present moment, creates an opportunity to search the real you of the present and yet opens the door to tomorrow and one's life purpose for every tomorrow. This redirects one's thinking from the painful reasons for dying to the healing reasons for living.

Join him in a family moment by creating your own Bucket List as well. Do the same process for yourself while you are participating as a support for him. You both will experience benefit.

This exercise brings appreciation to the process of creating, the valuing of our desires, and the reminder that life itself is a process. As an addict, what Murph is addicted to, which in turn is what seems to have all the power, can melt away in the light of the process.

You will find that Murph's list will evolve over time, which is as it should be. The ultimate goal is to know the comfort and strength of a defined purpose in life even if at first that purpose is to simply eat a solid meal once a day. Purposes at any stage of the process are the Lights that give direction and inspire the will power to move towards health and joy.

For now, Murph's life purpose is undefined, and the clarity of it seems impossible to discover. But it is there and has been there for all time. The journey to it is determined by his choices and his Free Will. We, as Spirit, will be there every step of the way offering treasure chests of gifts and enlightenment. Have him picture life as similar to his video games in that there will always be challenges and obstacles. We, of course, don't recommend violence in blasting those challenges away, but the metaphor can be helpful for him in picturing the road ahead

It is not an easy mission, but each effort at creating and updating a Bucket List can mean one more step forward. The Bucket List could be wildly creative to begin with. Anything goes! The power of it will be its ability to give grounding to an otherwise ungrounded path.

Start with the list, then refine it to the Top Ten. Next, have Murph prioritize it by putting what he would like to do first on the top. Then write the steps required to make it happen.

You are also doing a Top Ten and could model the process for him as you do it together. In this way, you are walking beside him, the key word being "beside." You cannot pull him from the front or push him from behind as his instinct could be to resist you. Rather, you will best serve by walking beside him from a position of your own grounding and the strength that comes from taking care of yourself first. Nurture your own body, heart, and soul.

Your heart-felt compassion is a sacred love walking beside him. Your love can be grounded and supported in your knowing that ultimately we all have a journey of our own with choices determined by our own Free Will. It is a Law of the Universe, and it is a responsibility that belongs to each person. It is never the responsibility of a parent or friend, lover, Angel, or even God to interfere with the Free Will of another. Be relieved of that burden.

Your sacred love can also be grounded in the knowing that what we fear the most is, in its finality, nothing to dread, even death. When anyone's physical life is brought to death's door, the soul lives on. The soul in an instant will find itself in the place of unconditional love where the spirit can recover, renew, and even reincarnate should it wish to. The soul and spirit of your loved one will always be connected to you, and it is sacred love that crosses all dimensions allowing it to carry on forever. It is never lost.

We understand that while you are on the earth plane you shudder to imagine the loss of a loved one, you grieve from even the thought of it, and life changes forever with the heartache when the physical life of a loved one ends. There is comfort, however, and there is healing and resurrection from heartbreak with the knowing that there is Eternal Life secured with eternal connection. There is a Forever Tribe existing in the presence of unconditional love.

So, prioritize the Top Ten, then set about taking one goal at a time starting with #1. If a snag brings a hitch to the accomplishment, move on to #2 knowing you can come back later to complete #1 if necessary. Along the way, you may see that the fireworks of desire on the Bucket List will present a strength of their own as they build upon the joy of accomplishment.

When the way to accomplish a goal seems impossible, keep it on the list. Ask for help. Pray for divine intervention and watch for miracles to happen. In all of life there will always be access to miraculous divine intervention. The source of that is in the dimension of Spirit which is well within reach merely by the asking and the allowing.

Communicating with Us is a source of miracles. Miracles make the impossible things possible and make the dark days passable even when the light seems to be a mere flicker. Miracles enable human frailty to take on the characteristics of strength and purpose. Miracles are Faith Builders and Gifts given of joy from supporting the journeys of souls who have chosen the earth plane experience for the value of learning and moving toward Love and Oneness.

Your spirit team hovers beside you wishing to be of service and wanting to remind you that You, Beloved of God, are precious in the Hands and the Heart of the Source of All That Is.

SPIRIT SPEAKS: *Purposes at any stage of the process are the Lights that give direction and inspire the will power to move towards health and joy.*

SPIRIT SPOTLIGHT: Bucket Lists

Until this message from Spirit, I always thought of the Bucket List as a way for retirees to get to doing what they have always wanted to do in life before it was too late. Now Spirit is suggesting that it be used as a tool to help any soul of any age overwhelmed by addiction and life to focus on purpose. I can see how perfect this tool is for increasing the likelihood for success in pulling out of addiction to build the win. The value of the Bucket List Exercise, for people with addictions and their loved ones, is worth a review.

It brings one to the present moment to search the real you of the Present, and yet it opens the door to tomorrow and one's entire life purpose for every tomorrow. This redirects one's thinking from the reasons for dying to the reasons for living.

Appreciation for the Present Moment, what could be more powerful than that for not only the addict but for any of us. Consider the value of living in the present and the freedom from not worrying, at least for the moment, about any mistakes from the past or any fears of the future. This is where we find clarity in the fog, which is critical before we can move forward. It opens the door then to look from today to tomorrow and more. I love the redirection, the move from the loop of the negative stories and nose-diving liabilities to the leap of a positive, newly created story.

The ultimate goal is to know the comfort and strength of a defined purpose. Purposes at any stage of the process are the Lights that give direction and inspire the will power to move toward health and joy.

• Creating a Bucket List is a practical way to define purpose because it's all about deciding what you want. On a grander scale, it is defining a life purpose which is about what you want, what brings you joy, what comes easily, what you could spend hours doing and still feel the passion.

• Creating the list is about making choices which reminds you that you have the power to choose; you are not a victim.

• The purpose gives you a destination and the motivation that having a destination brings.

• The purpose gives you a target. Something to go for increases the likelihood of success.
• Having a purpose brings comfort, strength, and value to your life.

• Defined purpose gives you Lights of direction and distracts you from the negative.

In contrast, purpose undefined feeds upon its own lack of clarity making what feels good or what one really wants impossible to see. That creates a reason for addiction rather than a reason to do the hard work of recovery. With the Bucket List project, there is purpose in the work of creating, there is purpose in the completion, and there is purpose in the new, next step of change.

Remember...***The rockets of desire on the Bucket List will present a strength of their own to build upon the joy of accomplishment.***

Creating the Bucket List and seeing it evolve, seeing targets achieved, and managing one piece at a time mirrors the process of life in a way that prevents the overwhelm. Valuing healthy desires, creating goals, clarifying, prioritizing, and breaking down the steps to accomplishment are vital steps which lead to letting go of the grip of our negative self-image, the self-medicating substances, and the illusion of power and fear. Paraphrasing Spirit, who we are today that we don't want to be, what we are addicted to, what seems to have all the power in our life, can melt away in the Light of the process.

The power of it will be its ability to give grounding to an otherwise ungrounded path.

It is often the relapse that is the un-doing of recovery, the un-sustainability of human effort to make it for the duration. The Bucket List will provide the grounding, involve the support of family for roots, and the involvement of Spirit will give the energy to keep it going.

You can join him in a family moment by creating your own Bucket List as well. Do the same process for yourself.

There is strength in numbers and camaraderie, a more likelihood of success with love and accountability, and more benefit when the entire family joins the activity. Besides, you need your own Bucket List Activity. You need your own help to keep pulling the wagon.

• *You will best serve from a position of your own grounding and the strength that comes from taking care of yourself first.*

• *Your heart-felt compassion is a sacred love that can be grounded in your knowing that ultimately we all have a journey of our own with choices determined by our own Free Will.*

• *Your sacred love can also be grounded in the knowing that what we fear the most is, in its finality, nothing to dread.*

• *Your love for the person with addiction is a driving force that could help them beyond measure on their healing path.*

• *Ask for help. Pray for divine intervention and watch for miracles to happen...merely by the asking and the allowing.*

Guides and Helpers from the Spirit world will not interfere with your life. They are, however, eagerly waiting for you to ask them for assistance. I imagine them sitting on the edge of their seats waiting to be invited to help, asking, "Have they called yet?"

Go ahead and ask. Then sit quietly and allow them to heal the deep, deep wounds inside, to pull out the daggers, to dissipate the fears, and to put love salve over the scar. The Universe wants you to heal so you'll recover the Joy. They are happy when you're happy. Besides, then you'll be a brighter Light for loving and serving others while co-creating the kind of consciousness that will touch the entire planet. Your love, especially when magnified by God's Unconditional Love, is enough to empower another being to drop their unhealthy addictions and move forward in a happier life. Be the Love. Be the Light.

From the Departed: A soul I know who is now passed, spent most of his life struggling with addictions and spoke to us from his own personal experience. His perspective from the Other Side is worth reading. He said to me:

Fear was the driver of my addictions. I feared that people I cared about would die. I feared that everyone would figure out that I was as dumb as my family told me I was. I feared that I was going to fall in a deep, dark hole and get stuck there forever.

Fear ruled, so then addictions ruled. Whatever was my compulsion at the moment became my source of power. Well, it felt like power. It was fake power because all it did was cover up the pain and desperation by distracting my focus away from myself and what was really going on inside.

The REAL power came in the moments when I felt the Love, the power that could help me become who I really wanted to be, to live how I really wanted to live.

Now I see it clearly. I'm telling you, go for the Love. Focus on Love like it was an addiction. Because when you least expect it, smile, you're on the Other Side! I don't want you to miss a minute of the power of love. From here where Spirit perspective sees the bigger picture, it truly is all about the love, love for yourself and love for every living thing.

Knowing it's all about love would make a huge difference in your day-to-day life. It would color your attitude, it would adjust your priorities, it would dissipate the other emotional extreme, fear.

Take it in so it can soothe your soul and heal your pain. It's authentic and it's empowering. It chips away at fear until fear finally disappears. Before you know it, you find yourself being the one giving the Love. Pass around the heart things. That feels powerful and real. Watch out, it's addictive.   *Love, Justin*

Steps for your healing generator:

Start with
the purpose in the task.
Discover the value of cooperation, learning, and interaction.
Move up to the satisfaction of completion,
the motivation of success.
Enjoy the view from the peak.

SECTION IV: FROM THE DEPARTED

Look In My Shoe

Arla has shed so many tears during these last two years. Each one is honored and sacred.

"I can't. I can't do it." Another panic attack. Arla just couldn't get herself out to the car to drive to work. It was too much. Everything closed in on her, and she could barely breathe. She slid to the floor in a heap, the look of terror mixed with desperation and conflict in her eyes. That's how she described it when she asked for a Reiki treatment.

Arla had just gone through the unthinkable, nine funerals in a little over one year, and now the unexpected death of her father. She had warned her husband years before, "If he goes before I do, just put me out to pasture."

Now she was in my office for Reiki support and healing. It seemed that every time we connected, someone dear to her had just passed including her mom, a favorite aunt, a not-so-favorite aunt, a cousin, a niece, two close friends, a neighbor, and a fellow teacher. All I could think of was how much I had seen her go through. So much loss either makes a person bitter or better—bitter for wrangling with so much pain or better for having been taken to the end of the line to discover what really matters.

Although tested to the hilt, Arla was still living her life with love and light. I had no doubt her now departed father would want to tell her that he is always with her in spirit and that he wants to help her through this tough time in any way that he can. We started our treatment, and right off the bat I could hear her dad's message. It was coming through with that Italian personality he was so well known for. This is what he said.

Stop being so sad. I know, I understand it's hard. Listen, live your life as you are living it now, and everything will be fine. It will. How am I? There's an adjustment to dying, but it's nothing I can't handle! I can have whatever I want here. And what I want is for YOU to be happy. You are the best kid ever. You are my kid, and I love you. Look for me in the shoe. I'll be with you every step of the way. You're my special lady.

I shared the message and Arla replied, "That's my dad for sure. Sounds just like him." I wondered what the reference to his shoe meant so she explained. Just a couple weeks before he died, she was visiting him and he had said to her, "If something should happen to me, I want you to look in my closet, get my shoes, and look inside."

She had forgotten about that until now. She said she would check. We continued with the treatment, and I asked Arla's dad if he had anything else he would like to say.

Tell her this: I have been hovering around you since I passed. You noticed my energy as you turned to see the rising sun. I told you to look for me in the Light. I want you to know that one day I won't be hovering so much. Not yet, but one day because the hovering doesn't allow room for the sunshine to get through. And I so want you to live in the sunshine.

Arla's dad moved back an another every moved forward. It was her Spirit Guide and he said, *"I am Peter, the Rock."* He continued.

Arla has shed so many tears during these last two years. Tell her that each one is honored and sacred. Arla will remember that in the Bible there is reference to God's eye being on each and every sparrow. It is a reminder that the tiny, or what may seem like the least of living beings, is precious to Spirit. Just as the feathers on every sparrow are important to God, so are Arla's tears. We know about the losses, we see the tears. Every single one is seen, understood, felt, and cherished.

I saw a clear image of a beautiful glass bottle with one tear reverently held inside. As that faded, I saw a picture of beautiful pink carnations and roses. I could hear Mary, the Mother of Jesus, saying that she, too, would be spending time with Arla. I could see the image of Mary as she shed tears for the loss of her son, Jesus. I remembered the tradition that where each of Mary's tears fell at the crucifixion cross, from each tear a pink carnation grew. The flowers are a reminder that each of Arla's tears are just as precious and life-giving.

I thanked all the energies of Spirit for the healing help so Arla could go on with her life. I could hear one final suggestion: Arla could use her crystals for support. She could use hematite for grounding and rose quartz for healing sadness and grief.

Two weeks later, Arla came in and told me the panic attacks had stopped right after her Reiki session, and she felt much better. She was able to get back to work with a renewed sense of purpose knowing that whatever she was called to do, she can always be the Light that she want to be.

What about the shoe? She looked in his shoes and found something very special. In one of the shoes was a piece of his personal jewelry he wanted her to have. It was his gold necklace. She knew exactly what it meant to him, and she will treasure it forever. Now she also knew the meaning of his message, *"I'll be with you every <u>step</u> of the way."*

SPIRIT SPEAKS: *Every tear is seen, understood, felt, and cherished.*

SPIRIT SPOTLIGHT: Life After Life
It is a blessing to be a part of the work of Reiki for holistic healing. Reiki creates a space and opportunity for another dimension beyond the physical allowing Spirit to appear with images, words, and feelings

of love and guidance. It is like being in the space of a vibrational frequency that merges the dimensions and allows us to be in the hallowed Other Side.

Hearing from Spirit or the departed and then having the resonance of from the multiple confirmations leaves me with no doubt whatsoever that there is life after death. The validating confirmations come with details and meanings that I don't always understand but when delivered through me, they make total and impacting sense to my clients. From having that experience, I know for certain there are departed souls, angels, and many identities of Spirit in another dimension who love to communicate with us and are eager to help us.

One client's grandpa spoke to us and asked, *"Would it inspire how you live to know that we departed loved ones are always with you?"*

For me, the inspiration is a rising up of courage, fearlessness, and a desire to allow Light to lead me. Yes, it inspires me to know that loved ones are with me, that their spirit energy loves and protects me. Their truth inspires me to be fearless about my beliefs and actions.

The departed grandpa continued, *"There is death after life and life after death."*

I had just been asking myself, "Why is there death after we have lived a full life? Every living thing goes through its life and then what? Just end up dead? Why go through all the bother of learning and getting wiser and working at all those relationships if death is the hopeless result? What's the point of it all? Does the end of life impact the meaning of life, and therefore, how I live it today? Are the departed with us? Does it matter?"

Grandpa chimed in with, *"These are the two great mysteries: Death after Life and Life after Death. And these great mysteries are just behind the greatest mystery of all which is Love.*

Then I saw a large rectangle standing vertically in my mind's eye. This is an image I have seen before. This time I asked, "What is the meaning of this symbol?"

"It is a window into the truth that we are multidimensional beings. When you see this symbol, it means you have just heard a Universal Truth, a window of insight regarding who we really are, an insight of understanding about the existence of the dimensions of body-soul-spirit."

The magical powers of love in this spiritual multiverse are yours to understand, yours to discover, yours to behold, yours to magnify, yours to deliver, and yours to hold.
Hugs.

I Can Fly!

It's OK to stop crying when you can… In looking for me you'll help the sad energy move along.

Souls connect with each other on the spirit energy level because we are all One including species to species. I have absolutely no doubts about that. Do our pets go to heaven? I have no doubts about that either. The evidence is in the true stories.

Friends since Junior High, Carla taught me a lot about dogs. I loved going to her house where there were always a couple of dogs, usually poodles. Carla loved her dogs and knew how to train them, which fascinated me. How did she do that? I loved watching her dogs do their tricks, adore their owner, and enjoy their life. She loved those four-legged creatures in a way I had never seen before.

I saw the good times of being a pet owner and then, of course, I got to see the inevitable tough times. Anyone who is a dog lover has undoubtedly asked God the same question that Carla asked, "Why do dogs have such short life spans?" Maybe they are old in the proverbial dog years, but way too young in human years to die. They cross over, our hearts break, and then we say, "I'll never have a pet again!" because losing them is too hard.

I have clients who come in for Reiki when they are healing from a loss. Whether their loss is a human or animal friend, pet or parent, spouse or child, the bereaved just want to know that their loved one is OK, that somehow they survived the transition, and they wonder if their loved one know hows much they are loved and missed.

Carla was feeling all those things because her dog, Ridget, just died. It wasn't that long ago when Carla brought Ridget home as a puppy, and they both bonded in that special way. He fit into the family along with the family bird. They had such good times together. Then there it was, that way too short doggie life span. Inevitably, Ridget faced old age, with all of

its physical disabilities, and then Carla's dearly beloved came to the end of his earthly life. As expected, she was heartbroken. Again. No matter how many times one goes through the loss of a pet, it is always a terrible experience.

Wanting to somehow bring comfort to my friend, I wondered if Spirit would have a message I could share or maybe some wisdom or insight about death and crossing over. Maybe Ridget himself was around and would have a message to give to Carla. I quieted down and began to listen and communicate with Spirit. "Spirit, I am open to receive. Is Ridget around?"

Ridget was there, available, and he did indeed have a touching and comforting message for Carla. I'll write it here just as I heard it. It is so beautiful and so well said.

Yes, I want to send a message. I love you! I loved my life with you and my life in my earth body. I loved the crunchies. I loved the family. I loved my bed and toys. I loved my spot. I loved my yard. I loved you mom and dad. I loved doing tricks. I loved my bird. I loved my bandana.

Thank you for crying for me. It's OK though to stop crying when you can. Tell your heart I'm OK. Better than OK. Better than you might imagine.

Just as pens stop writing, our earthly bodies stop working. The pen is still a pen though. Just maybe out of ink. I'm still me. Me in a spirit energy. A pen is a pen. A dog is a dog. A dog runs out of earth life but a heart never runs out of love. I will love you in ways you never knew.

Look for me in the fields as a flying bird, flying butterfly, flying dragonfly. Because I can fly now. Watch for me and learn about energy life. When our body stops living like when a pen runs out of ink and stops working, we have an energy life that never runs out of ink.

What can you do and how can you live without me? Lift up your head and look for me. Because in looking for me you'll help the sad energy move along. Then the sad energy will become love energy.

So many living things need your love and help right now. Love is help, and help makes a difference between being able to carry on or just letting the ink dry up. It's better to carry on, learn more and love more. It's all about the love.

That was God's idea, and God knows best. It's a good idea to Love. You can't just make it up like you can just make up a game, or make up a name or a word. Love was created by God and is a gift to everyone who will receive it, and give it.

There you have it. Thanks for loving me and for the best life ever. You think it's fun flying on a four-wheeler. Wait until you fly without it! Now that's cool.

The bigger part of life is what happens outside the earth body. Life in a body is short and limited. Outside of the body we are back to being energy. Now that's big, and that's your soul. Love always, Your Ridget

P.S. You'll know it's me by the song I sing. You know, the howl. how-ooooo.

SPIRIT SPEAKS: *It's all about the love... Love was created by God and is a gift to everyone who will receive it and give it. There you have it.*

SPIRIT SPOTLIGHT: Why do our pets have short lifespans?

Animals in all of the Animal Kingdom are extraordinary to behold. They are miraculous gifts to us. The creatures of the air, the oceans, and fields have so much to teach us on the human plane. Their lives give us the opportunity to observe and learn about all their stages of life, their birthing, enjoying fullness, then dying, all the while experiencing their unconditional love as we go. So why do they have such short life spans?

You've heard of the concept "Dog Years." It's as if they pack seven years worth of life into just one year. Toby, my horse friend, says that animals have short life spans so they can live big. Their life is too short to spend it on anything other than love.

Maybe that is enough for one lifetime. Well, not enough for pet lovers because we want more time with them, more life. There is nothing easy or simple about grieving the death of a pet. Right up there with needing oxygen, we need to know that our departed pets are OK, that they got there OK, and that they are still with us in spirit. Hearing their spirit messages back to us from heaven lets us know for certain that yes, yes, and yes.

I know for certain that the souls of animals are eternal just like the souls of humans not only because I have heard from so many over the years with confirmations but also because it makes sense. And I know for certain that we can communicate with them between heaven and earth. That, too, makes sense.

All species and all dimensions have many things in common including the essence of us which binds us together. We cross the species barrier and the heaven barriers because of that same essence. That essence is energy. Biologically it is the electrons and protons, and spiritually it is the life force of the soul energy.

Life on the physical plane is but a limited manifestation of who we really are which is Spirit. Our infinite soul energy is much larger than the physical body confinement, just like with animals. Our Spirit part of us is much larger than life and lives forever.

That is how our pets come across when they bring us their messages from the other side. Big, expanded, grateful for their earth family, and happy, just like Ridget. My own beloved chihuahua, Scooch, confirmed that same understanding. Right after she died, I was talking to my horse friend and said to him, "Toby, did you know my Scooch died?" Toby replied:

Yes. And I know it doesn't feel good, and you want to feel better. Talking to me can help you feel better. Also get rest. Don't try to do too much. Reach for quietness, and only do things you like as much as you can.

Remember we are all here for you to give you time, and conversation, and understanding. Scooch is happy. Scooch is loved and receiving love and accolades for her bravery, strength, endurance and love. All the animals of the world care. We are a community.

As Toby was talking, suddenly there was a bright spotlight shining in my face. It was sparkly and kaleidoscope like, flowing and blinking brightly like intense fireworks in my mind's eye. Then right in the middle of the light show, Scooch's face appeared. She was smiling and excited. It looked like she was trying to do a selfie and was moving her head to fit in the screen, trying to get her happy, excited face in the frame.

She was so excited she couldn't sit still. She was jumping around like a little puppy. She was saying "See me? See me? I'm happy! I'm happy!" She kept putting her paw up tapping clumsily across the screen trying to wave to me.

Then she excitedly said, "Look at this! I get to see myself in the movies." She was showing me what looked like a film strip of the old home movie type, flickering black and white film with those gear-hole edges on both sides. She was showing me movies of when she was a puppy. She was so cute. Oh my, how precious.

Her soul and her love were large enough and bright enough to break through the density of the earth plane that she had just left to let me know she was OK.

How do I know it was her and not just me making it up? I have no doubts whatsoever. I recognized the energy of her. I knew it was her because of how it felt and the resonance in my heart. You can't make resonance just happen, just like you can't make yourself have goosebumps. It was her all right.

Our connection with Spirit is eternal. The love we feel in the animal and human connection is likewise infinite. Our animal companions are spiritual companions in all directions of time.

Connect with the love of your deceased loved ones
by looking for them where they are now and not where
they were when walking on earth.

Migraines.
I died first, so here I am.

"I've had a migrane for 3 ½ months! I go to the chiropractor once a week, every two weeks I get acupuncture, I keep going to the doctor, and all he does is give me more medicine that makes me crazy, and now they're going to do an MRI."

That explains what Shari said as she walked through the door, "I'm here for a treatment, and I'm hoping you can help me. I'm a mess."

I asked, "What do YOU think is causing the migraines?"

"It's just stress. I know it is. So I'm on these crazy meds for this constant terrible headache, and yesterday I got stopped for speeding. I was going 45 in a 35 but not only that, my rear tail light was out plus I was in a construction zone. Oh man, it's a good thing they didn't give me a breathalyzer or a drug-alyzer test! I'd have failed, not from alcohol but from pills. I'm not taking these stupid drugs anymore."

I asked, "Other than this encounter with the officer, tell me about the stress. What's going on?"

"Well my sister's husband just got diagnosed with kidney failure. And my neighbor dropped dead last week. He seemed just fine, was out and about as usual, and then there he was lying on the floor, gone. I was in the house when they tried to revive him, and it was just awful. Besides that, my son broke up with his girlfriend, and now he wants to come home and live with us."

I wondered out loud, "Are you an empath?" Shari looked at me blankly and ask, "What is that?"

"Well, an empath is a person who is very empathetic, which is a good thing, but sometimes it can go to the point of taking on other peoples' feelings and troubles. Do you ever do that?"

"You got that right. I sure do," she said.

Reiki could help with this. I jumped right in. Shari's Spirit Guide jumped right in as well. I felt a loving presence and enthusiastic spirit energy so I asked who was with us. I heard, *"I'm Shari's Guardian Angel. I am not literally an angel, but I made an agreement with Shari that if I died before she did, then I promised that I was going to be her guardian angel. I died first so here I am. I love her and want to help."*

"OK then. I am so glad that you are here," I said.

I did a Reiki Byosan Scan for information about Shari's energy field, and I decided to double check my sense of things by using the pendulum. The same imbalances showed up. I knew where I needed to focus the Reiki work: the sacral chakra (abdomen) and then the crown chakra (head) I started the Reiki and listened closely for spirit guidance and found myself conversing once again with Shari's Guardian Angel. I scribbled down some notes so I could remember to tell Shari everything at the end of the session.

I was happy to see Shari looking totally relaxed by the end of the treatment. The look of migraine pain was gone. I gently checked in with her.

"How are you doing?" Although appearing a bit groggy, she quickly said, "My headache is so much better." She said she was awake enough to hear what Spirit had to say about consider her migraines.

Shari has known me to receive divine messages, and she replied right away with a solid "Yes!"

"These are suggestions from your Guardian Angel, a lovely personality and a female energy who said she promised you that if she died first, she was going to be your Guardian Angel."

Shari knew exactly who I was talking about and was really pleased to hear from her. I began to explain the three things that her Guardian

Angel offered for stress relief and in turn for migraine relief. All three exercises make sense and could help anyone to release that headache grip.

1. Do this: Breathe in through your feet and your crown.

We normally breathe through our mouth and nose, not our feet and head, so I suggested we try that together. "Breathe normally in and out of your nose while at the same time imagine also breathing in through the bottoms of your feet." We did that together breathing in through our feet and taking the breath all the way up to our abdomen, holding it there, then breathing out taking that energy back down and out through our feet. I said, "Imagine breathing in the solid energy of the earth and spreading that energy through all your cells as you breathe out. We'll do that 5 times."

Then we did the same thing breathing through the crown chakra which is at the top of your head. "Breathe normally in and out of your nose while at the same time imagine also breathing in through the top of your head. Imagine breathing in through your crown all the way down to your heart, hold it there, then breathe out taking that energy back up and out through the top of your head. On your next inhale, imagine breathing in the white Light and Love of God and spreading that energy through all your cells as you breathe out. We'll do that 5 times."

As I explained it to Shari while we practiced together, the more sense it made that this could break open the cycle of the relentless migraines and release the built up stress and stagnation of energy in her body. I drew a picture so she would remember how to do it at home: grounding through the feet, opening up through the crown, and balancing all the chakras in between as the energy is pushed through the abdomen and heart chakras.

2. This second exercise was for Shari's closed Sacral Chakra, the center of creativity. The message was this: *"You must take the*

time to be creative. What is it that you love to do? And are you doing what you love? Something you love so much you could spend hours doing it, something with colors, something that you can build and create, design and fashion?"

Shari's face looked blank with the realization that she wasn't doing anything creative at all. How did she ever lose that? She used to be very creative all those years as an elementary school teacher. What happened over time that she gave all her energy away to worrying about others? And what happened that she left no time for doing things that she loved? What impact might there be to return to moments of joy and creativity? She said she would find something creative to get involved in.

3. Shari's Guardian Angel ended her advice saying, "Now one more thing, and ask your Guardian Angel, me, to help you with this because it won't be easy at first. Here it is: Consider setting some boundaries around your empathic personality. You decided long ago to be empathetic because that's how you wanted to live out your purpose. Well, what if we took that to another level? What if you loved and served people, but then could go home then and let them have their own journey? Let me repeat that. What if you loved and served people, but then could go home and let them have their own journey?"

As I summarized for Shari, I wrote this down: BREATHE. CREATE. ASK for HELP. She agreed to try it. I can't wait to hear how it's going. Imagine how wonderful to rid her life of migraines, drugs, MRI's, and speeding tickets.

SPIRIT SPEAKS: *What is it that you love to do? And are you doing what you love?*

SPIRIT SPOTLIGHT: Breathing in Heaven

There are many breathing techniques available to experiment with in order to discover what works best. Research the Energy Medicine and Alternative Therapies such as Yoga, Meditation, or Vibrational Healing. Test them all to find the one that you like, believe in, and will actually use. Nearly every energy treatment stresses attention to the breath using the cleansing breath, the releasing breath, and the relaxing breath. In Reiki, we talk about breathing through our hands and our heart. In Quantum Touch, we breathe to "run" the energy. In Energy Codes, we breathe to activate our circuits. In chiropractic settings with the Associative Awareness Technique, it is called Reflexercise. They are all excellent stress reduction, healing, breathing methods.

The focus on specific breathing techniques is for the benefit, as in Shari's case, to help relieve the stress and headaches. It is magical that something as simple and natural as breathing could bring so much relief. The exchanging of oxygen and carbon dioxide within our lungs is amazing in itself, and the fact that it happens automatically keeps it so simple. I marvel how the Plant Kingdom comes to our rescue with its part in the big breath exchange by taking our carbon dioxide and turning it into oxygen for us. Breathing is a miraculous, biological event when you stop to think about it.

Plus, it is phenomenal in the way it leads to connecting to Spirit as one of the basic steps. Focusing on breathing takes you to that place where you brain slows down so your connection can begin, that astonishing place of complete focus and deep peace where you hardly realize you are breathing at all. Right there you are lifted to a celestial place.

My mystical side loves to question, and I have asked God about breath and breathing at different times. "Do you breathe in Heaven? Is the power to breathe part of that alpha, omega, and meta (beyond), to infinity and beyond?" Spirit replied:

There is no inhale and exhale in heaven, no. The life of the body begins and ends with the first and last breath. The life of the <u>soul</u> begins and ends with pure being-ness, the manifestation of eternal existence. Being-ness is the vibrational essence that can create whatever it wants or doesn't want while having no need to be sustained by breathing. It is sustained by its nature which is eternal vibrational essence. Because there is no need to be sustained by breath, being-ness is eternal-ness with no beginning and no ending.

So breathing stops but creativity doesn't. "What about the saying 'The Breath of God' which in context was about the power of breath to be the means of creation, how God creates. Does God breathe?"

Dear One, we are happy to discuss breath and breathing. It is most assuredly a human, animal, and plant characteristic of the physical realm found throughout the planet. Its purpose is to exchange air, and this is quite a miracle in itself. But does it go beyond?

In the beyond, there is breathing should you define breathing as an exchange. An exchange exists between souls which you would call telepathy. Telepathy is "breathing" in the 5th dimension. It exists to support 5th dimensional life, to give soul life color and meaning. It would be so quiet without it. Not fruitful, not interesting, not sustainable. The breath of God is the telepathy of God and is the Creation of God. The creative process is a gift that keeps on giving. It never dies. It truly is the alpha, omega, and meta.

———————————

Exercise: The Four Breaths

This is a great breathing technique for using breath as more than an exchange of air. This is how it works: Take four breaths, one for each of the following: grounding, cleansing, calming, and opening your heart. The cycle is four breaths, but you may want to take more than one breath at each level of the cycle. Repeat the cycle four times.

The <u>grounding</u> breath means that you breathe as if the breath was drawing air and energy up from the floor beneath you, the ground, the dirt, the earth, and the planet into the soles of your feet and up through your body. It feels stable, safe, strong and connects you to solid ground.

The <u>cleansing</u> breath feels as if the air you breathe in fills your entire body. As you breathe out, the rushing and flowing air picks up and takes with it anything you want to have taken away, lifted off, blown through, let go of.

The <u>calming</u> breath goes as deep into your abdomen as you can. Breathe in deeply, hold it there for 3 seconds, then exhale. When you let go and exhale, your shoulders automatically fall and your body releases tension from every muscle and joint.

The final breath for <u>opening your heart</u> is inhaling directly to your heart. The breath collects there in your heart, hold it as long as you can, and imagine the exhale breaking through any walls or protective barriers that have closed your heart off. On the first breath, let the exhale break through with power. For subsequent breaths, let the exhale end softly in relief.

No More About My Legs
You are not cheating on me.

"I don't want the conversation to be about my legs anymore. I'm so tired of it. I want to be with my friends and talk about other things. And dance! And ride my bike!"

Sue Ann was telling me about the life impacting issue going on for her as she hobbled with her cane to the chair. She explained that she experiences both numbness and involuntary movement in her legs and sometimes her arms. "It's been going on long term, and the docs are calling it neuropathy or maybe restless legs, they don't know. None of that pile of medicines was helping a bit though! So now the doctor thinks something else is going on."

"What does she think is going on?" I asked.

"Oh the nurse wouldn't say. She just said the doctor will talk about it at your next appointment."

Nothing like being left hanging as your life goes on with this constant, what shall we call it, cramping of her life style? She's had a lifetime of other tough physical problems, quite a list really, but none as long lasting and irritating at this one.

As soon as I started her Reiki treatment, my whole body became unsteady. I asked for Spirit's help and used the Reiki symbols to clear the unbalanced energy and move it out of the room.

As I stood at her feet, I felt very little pulse. I imagined and asked for white light to pass through her left foot and leg, up to her crown, around her head, and then back down her right side through the bottom of her right foot and from there cycle around her entire body. I stayed there until I could feel a pulse and sensed that a circulation of energy was getting through. Sue Ann said she was shocked because she could feel her feet for the first time in ages. The numbness was gone, and she could actually feel her toes.

On the spot, I felt inspired to give her an assignment to do at home to help her healing continue after the appointment: <u>Grounding exercises</u>. We did it together to practice.
   • Breathe in and imagine the energy going UP your Right leg; breathe out and the energy goes back down through your left leg into the earth.
   • Reverse. Breathe in and imagine the energy going UP your Left leg; breathe out and the energy goes back down through your right leg into the earth.
   • Lastly, breathe up through BOTH legs; breathe out and back down through both legs into the earth.

She liked how she felt after doing the breathing and said she would do it at home. Continuing with the Reiki treatment, I began the work of balancing her chakras starting with her solar plexus and heart. It was while working right there that I could hear a Spirit begin to talk. I recognized the presence as a departed loved one but I didn't know who. Spirit said:

She feels so unworthy. I'll show you what I mean. Ask her this: "If you fell in a pond, what is the first thing you would say?" You will see by her response how undeserving she feels.

I suspected she would say a put-down of herself like, "How could I be so darn stupid?" Then I kept hearing something about *"She needs to talk to me.   There is some unfinished business she needs to talk about."* Maybe that's what was closing up her throat chakra. I had noticed no energy movement there.

I asked Sue Ann quietly, "Is there someone who has crossed over that you have unfinished business with? Like you feel responsible for something? Or you need to talk to them and get something resolved? There is a presence here, a soul who really wants to talk to you."

"Yes, there is someone. I know exactly who it is. I am cheating on him."

She teared up and started to cry as the story began to trickle out. "It's my ex- husband who has died but I feel like I'm cheating on him because I'm with another man. This man asked me to marry him, and I just stood there and couldn't find a single word to answer him because I was numb with confusion and guilt and abiding love for – someone else. He immediately said to me, 'Oh sorry. I guess my timing was off.' But I told him no, no, that's not it. I just didn't know what to say."

Inside, Sue Ann was overwhelmed with guilt. "It's so silly," she said. "He's gone and what does it matter? But I love him and I just can't let go. He has obviously let go of me. He can do it. Why can't I?"

I asked, "What would you like to say to him? Let's talk to him right now."

"Does he still love me? Is he mad that I am cheating on him?"

He answered: *I love you. I always will. I will love you forever. We will always be in the same tribe. Forever. Do you know how long that is? It's forever. My dear one, it's not that I have let go of you. It's that my love is not something I hold on to. It's something that illuminates from me, and it's free to go everywhere. That's how it works here on the other side. My love is not just directed to one person. It's illuminating and touches many."

I could see the picture of a man with a big heart that was just beaming with a brilliant white light of love. He lovingly continued. *You are not cheating on me. And you don't have to let go of me. Just let the energy of your love for me illuminate from you to everyone it might touch. Use the energy of "lost love" to illuminate love energy. You don't have to aim it at anyone in particular unless you want to. Just let it shine from you. And those around you will feel it and receive it. Can you imagine that?*

"How can I possibly do that?" she asked through her sobbing and wiping away of tears. I heard:

Ask for help. Ask and we will. Let this be your mantra: Help me and heal me so that my love can illuminate like a light from me.

The room was flooded with an instantaneous infusion of resonance, self-forgiveness, acceptance, enlightenment, compassion, freedom, and love. The light of it literally filled the room. We spent time in silence taking it all in. Then we chatted a little more with her departed loved one. Then more silence taking it all in.

Finally, Sue Ann was able to speak again. She said with resolution as she wiped more tears away, "I have a celebration to plan. It's time to accept and celebrate an engagement and marriage to a wonderful man. He is truly a gift to me. I honestly feel like I am free now to love him and love my life."

"And love yourself," I added. "It's time to love others but it's equally important to love yourself and give time and attention to what makes you happy."

Sue Ann is on a new path now. As we were wrapping up our time together, I wrote down the two assignments, the grounding exercises and her new mantra. Then Spirit reminded me of the pond question. I wasn't sure I wanted to break the lovely atmosphere of love and compassion, but I told Spirit I would ask her the pond question. So I asked, "If you were to slip and fall into a pond, what is the first thing that you would say?"

Sue Ann said, "I would say "Oh darn! I was so stupid!"

Just as we expected. I said to Sue Ann, "Oh dear. We knew you would be hard on yourself. So let's practice this. Let me give you some new words you could consider saying. What if you could rephrase your response to, 'Oh darn. But now I get to change my clothes.' Can you see the difference? It's not about hitting yourself on the head for being so stupid. It's about—correction. Just put on a clean, dry set of clothes and live on." Practice that approach.

"It's time to celebrate," I said. "Get walking in the truth of your path and your legs will follow you."

SPIRIT SPEAKS: *Help me and heal me so that my love can illuminate like a light from me.*

⌁

SPIRIT SPOTLIGHT: Alignment In Relationships

Throughout my experiences with clients having decisions to make about relationships, Spirit has given many guiding words. I picked out some to share here from various situations. Read sacred guidance offered for a variety of circumstances yet relevant for us all.

Relationships are primary ways of learning many lessons. It is to your benefit to have pleasure in the midst of the challenges that relationships can bring, so expect challenges but also expect times when your feelings are satisfied. That is your lamp post to follow, your sign to continue. The challenges need not deter you, and the good times of connection, joy, and laugher will fuel your Light rather than dim it.

When a difficulty arises, surrounding a situation with plenty of <u>preparatory</u> positivity will always be of benefit. That could be sending ahead positive energy in prayer, heart-felt intentional thought, sending Reiki, and in the asking for Spirit guidance and help.

How to know the wisest actions? Alignment for any situation or relationship is best achieved with letting go of preconceived wishes or expectations. Be "present" while at the same time leave all outcomes to the Universe, to your understanding of a power that is in alignment with your Higher Self, God, and the Spirit team you invite to give you guidance.

Twin Flame relationships are for the benefit of both twins. The relationship blossoms in the realization that love abounds in the presence of unconditional acceptance and in the allowing of each heart flame to bloom in its own garden. Isn't it wonderful that the sunshine of one is available to help the growing of another no matter the dimension of time or space? Love and attending to matters of the heart crosses all boundaries and veils.

Every soul benefits from the adoring acceptance and endearing freedom given from the heart of another. Attend to your relationships with grace and those efforts will be worthwhile to nurture both flames. When it is specific actions that you may be looking for, check in with your heart and ask, "What does my flame need today?" You can never go wrong with simply giving time, attending to a moment, and feeling the heart love.

When one's wish and desire is to be in alignment, there is benefit to asking for guidance each day. When you do so, you develop a trust that things are as they are meant to be, or in other words, things happen that have purposes beyond what we can know in the moment, or purposes we can learn more about from the act of seeking, and purposes that build upon what we realize and understand from our life's collection of experience and wisdom.

Poems will be written from vulnerability, wisdom will be learned from challenges, and seeking will find resonance in answers. Therefore, things are as they are meant to be for many purposes including protection, lessons to learn, or for service to others for the benefit of one or the benefit of many.

In this case, your friends will ponder their dilemma and they will discover that yes, things are as they are meant to be. In fact, many times it takes great effort on the parts of Guides and Angels to perfectly and masterfully bring together energies of Spirits and Souls who can benefit, learn from, and be protected by the very act of their lives intersecting.

When that intersection has produced a contrast of emotions and a complexity of on-going feelings, there is an opportunity to seek, learn, and grow. The depths and heights, the closeness and distance, the richness and loss are contrasts not easy to manage. So consider this option: deal with contrasts as you deal with pain. As you lean into the feelings they evoke, you realize that contrast and pain take you to a place you may have never been before, at least at this level at this time in your life. They take you to an opportunity you have never had before to find a new depth of receiving, giving, opening, and allowing.

There, in the depths of contrast, ask for Divine help by saying, "I am open to receive whatever it is that will help me walk through the opportunities of contrast so that I may become even more in touch with who I am and who I can be."

As you experience depths of contrast, you could realize even more contrast as you ask, "What could be worse?   What could be better?"   Ask, "Will this crush me or will I stand upon it to find a perspective that is from a Higher Place?"   You get to choose.

Do not despair.   There are no wrong choices.   There are merely more challenging choices than others.   See where you can find the Divinity of You, the Divinity in You, and the Divinity around You.   The resolution will lead you to a deeper place and a higher place, both deserving of a jeweled crown.

Brave Ones, what leads us to fall upon our knees
may lead us to notice the nature of our wings.

I Turned My Phone Off
How do you mend a broken heart?

Few challenges in life can compare to the devastation of a parent losing a child especially when the anguish is magnified by the many "should have, could have, and why didn't I see it" regrets? Emma had just graduated from high school days before her fatal drug overdose.

It had been two years ago but rather than time healing the grief, time had instead taken Emma's mom, Jill, to dark places. The wretchedness of the misery, guilt, and constant reruns of what happened had obviously taken a terrible toll. She came in for Reiki to try to reduce the stress, and her first words were, "My child is gone and I don't know what has become of her. I can't feel her. I want to but she's just not there."

I listened to the cry for help and was glad she came in for Reiki. It turned out to be a powerful session. Into the treatment, in the sacred place of quietness and reverence, Spirit said:

"Healing will not be found in only asking the questions about what happened, Healing is not just in hearing the answers. Healing is in the letting go. That, of course, does not mean don't ask the questions. Do by all means. Ask all your questions and ask for all the help you need. In fact, let us work with the questions first, and then we will lead you in a healing experience to support you in the difficult part of letting go."

Many spiritual beings were present in the room bringing their love, support, wisdom, and healing. The spirit of Buddha was present, Quan Yin, Jesus, Archangels Raphael and Michael, and then, of course, the spirit of Emma.   Using techniques of Reiki, I intentionally ask for celestial intervention to create a safe place and surround us with energetic protection dedicated to the healing of the wounds of grief.

The soul of Emma was shy about speaking with us. She came forward with her shoulders lowered and head bowed. I asked her how she was doing, and she said that she felt shame for her behavior at the end of her life and unworthy of her Mom's love and forgiveness.

I relayed that to Mom, and we spent several minutes in a conversation of each sharing their feelings. When Jill asked despairingly, "Where are you? I haven't felt you around since you died, I haven't heard anything from you or had any sense of your presence. Are you there?"

Emma's look was one of "I'm so sorry." She picked up what looked like a cell phone and started dialing. The digits that I could see were m-o-m. She looked up and said, "Mom, I was so ashamed that I turned my phone off."

I described what I was seeing and hearing to Jill. "Emma is using a cell phone, and she's trying to call you." I could see the tears of resonance begin to trickle down Jill's cheeks. She said, "Emma and I talked on our cell phones every day. More than anything else, I miss those calls. I look at my phone every day and wish that I could hear from her. " That moment of resonance and connection was the beginning of healing.

Mom continued with heartfelt love asking questions, sharing what she wanted Emma to know, and giving her the gift of unconditional caring and forgiveness. Within a few minutes, Emma was able to receive that love and forgiveness. I could see her lift her head up and see all the spirit support around her. She saw souls she recognized who had departed before her. She began to feel the love.

Before long, she was able to say, "I'll turn my phone on. Watch for the hearts." Now Mom and others on the earth plane will hear from her and feel a connection with her soul—something Mom, family, and friends have been longing for and needing.

I asked Spirit for suggestions for how Mom could heal going forward, things she could do every day, ways to re-route the grief energy without taking away from the necessary process. Spirit recommended these things:

- *Breathe. Breathe through your heart chakra. Breathe deeply for relief.*

- *Involve yourself whenever possible in doing things you enjoy. It will take some time to remember what makes you happy, and it will be some time before joy comes back into your vocabulary, but try, and each effort will bring you one step closer to healing.*

- *Give Emma your love every day. Your love and forgiveness will help her soul to heal.*

- *Ask continuously for help from your spirit team. You get to choose your team. They are waiting to be invited, and they will help in many ways to love you through this and to support you through the healing process.*

- *Read books that remind you that our soul lives forever, that communicating with souls who have crossed over is indeed possible, it happens, and it helps. Read the testimonies and evidence that communication is real.*

- *Carry a grounding stone or something of Emma's in your pocket to remind you to be grounded and stay connected to the earth plane while you are still wearing your physical shoes, to remind you that it will be OK that you are here while she is there, for now, and to remind you that her spirit is with you.*

- *When you feel the grief, place it respectfully in a box and lift it up to God. God will put His hands under yours to help you lift it, and to help you know that He is with you. Lift it up for the letting go. There are many stages to grief so this can be done a number of times over the days ahead until one day you will realize you have released the grief and have more room for the love.*

Your "letting go" is you making a sacrifice of your grief by courageously offering it up to let it be taken from you, to release it to Archangel Michael so that he may transmute it into energy that is positive Love and Light. Letting go is for the purpose of your healing which will benefit you, Emma, and everyone around you.

No one grieves the same so no one can tell you how to do it. Release the pressure of expectations you put on yourself or that others may put on you to grieve or not grieve in a certain way. Let others have their journey with as much grace as you can give, and always stand up for and take care of yourself. Be gentle, compassionate, and forgiving toward yourself first. In time you will realize that you have strength to be gentle and compassionate toward others.

You are still on the earth plane, and you have a purpose and perhaps many purposes for being here. We all thank you for doing what you need to do to heal. Letting go of the grief is not letting go of your daughter or her memory. It is letting go of the depths of loss that paralyze and inhibit you from living. It is letting go of the natural sadness that in time is no longer helpful. It is letting go to open up space in your soul where Emma and her memory can rest and remain, always surrounded with a peace that represents the love that you shared and will always share. You are connected forever in a tribe that will always be your family.

I shared Spirit's wisdom, and then before she left, I reminded Jill that Emma said to watch for the hearts. Already Jill felt the confirmation as she told me about the hearts on Emma's note that she left. Jill's hand reached up and cradled the heart on the necklace from her. Emma will do her best to show her mom signs that her soul lives on, and that her love is forever.

SPIRIT SPEAKS: *Letting go of the grief is not letting go of your daughter or her memory. It is letting go of the depths of loss that paralyze and inhibit you from living.*

SPIRIT SPOTLIGHT: Signs

In a few days, Jill touched base with me. She felt a little better and hoped it was true that Emma's soul was going to show her more signs. She wrote, "When Emma died, I gave up all hope. I always believed God would protect my kids and keep them from harm. I had no doubt about it, but then Emma died, and my believing stopped. I will wait for more signs from Emma. This would also make me more of a believer."

My heart ached with Jill, and I thought about all of those times in life when our pure and trusting beliefs take a hit. The rug gets pulled out from under us, our faith fractures, and it feels as if our very core and foundation gets shattered. How do you ever pick up the pieces again? How do you even want to?

From all spans of time, history records tragedy upon tragedy. From all those times, when trust was broken and beliefs were shattered, what happened next? Rebuilding, restoring, reassembling.

We may not be able to do it ourselves at first, but we do get to decide to rebuild, for us and for our beloved. Eventually we will even once again be able to reach out to others including those who get to live their normal life while we are trying to survive our fractured world.

Asking questions, seeking wisdom, letting time take its healing course, allowing the love of others to be the glue are all part of the restoration.

Spirit says:

How does one climb the mountain back to belief? It is a journey best recognized by personal experience, each person's way being their own. Most likely it will be a meandering one with steps going forward, backward, and sideways. We cannot decide or prepare for what is our way or theirs.

For some, it may seem there could never be enough signs from their beloved. Their needs feel like a sieve. Signs just keep flowing through, and it is difficult to maintain the faith that will plug up the holes of grief. Keep asking, watching and eventually you will notice a filling. Until then, acknowledge the signs you have and find a way to give your own signs. Send out signs of love by creating memorials to honor, foundations to support a cause, or send care packages to comfort. There are many possibilities.

During that climb back to belief, consider journaling. You will see in writing the markers that signpost healing. You will notice that you were able to get out of bed, get through the next moment. Journal the evidence that you got through several moments. Then one day you will find something to live for and eventually see enough signs to sigh rather than scream, to breathe rather than squeezing tightly, holding on for dear life. Then one day you will discover you can get through an entire day without checking out.

As time journeys on while you hold dear the signs and give your own signs, with faith building from journaling, the fog will clear and it will be enough to make it. One day you will feel better.

It may take days, months, and years but one day, and then many days after, belief will once again be a solid foundation to stand on.

Take all the time and ask for all the signs that you need. The signs may show up even without the asking, but it helps to be a believer in the possibilities and to notice the synchronicities.

Before my mom died, I asked her what signs was she going to send our way and at the time she didn't know for sure but we decided that dragonflies could work. I had made her a quilt from her hand sewn dragonfly patches, bought her dragonfly jewelry, and took dragonfly photos. So the morning after she passed, I was opening the screen door of my sister's home and there fluttering behind the screen was the largest, most magnificent dragonfly I had ever seen. I wasn't looking for a sign, but I couldn't miss that one! Since then, I see them all the time hovering in front of my car windshield, following me on my walk around the lake, or landing on the wildflowers in front of me. They have shown up everywhere I have been, in Pennsylvania, New York, North Carolina, and Florida. Way to go, Mom.

How do you know the signs are really signs of the presence of a departed loved one, or whatever you are seeking like the guidance of God, or the influence of Spirit? The most accurate sign is your own feelings. You will know within yourself because of the resonance in your heart. For me, the sign that never fails is goosebumps. You can't <u>make</u> goosebumps happen. If you get goosebumps or a positive feeling like, "That's it!" then that's it. Believe it.

Feeling grief myself, I asked Jesus, "How do YOU mend a broken heart?" Jesus said:

I would take your hand. I would take both of your hands and hold them in mine. I would feel your pain, and you would feel my love. The sharing would help ease the pain. Go ahead and share your pain because when you can tell the story of how you feel, the story of the loss of your loved one, who they were, what they meant to you, it helps. You will feel my unconditional love for you, and that love will be a salve to heal your grieving heart. As you feel the love of those around you, it can soothe your broken heart.

Sometimes there are moments of miracles, sometimes there are flashes of hope, but mostly there are just steps. When you feel overwhelmed from grief, imagine falling into arms larger than yours. When your broken heart takes every ounce of energy from you, breathe and let the touch of love be the salve. When you are struggling to put even one foot forward, imagine hands of support lifting you up. When you can stand, imagine the rock under you, the hand of Spirit above you, and there you are, remembering you are the Beloved.

Grief takes us deeply to the place where the only language left is the language of the soul. Spirit says,

The language of the soul will bring the resonance
that speaks deeply, the resonance that can't be made
up merely from your efforts to understand life.

Understanding may not always come from effort.
It may simply come from our soul to yours.

Healing on Both Sides of the Veil
Eventually you will awaken to a purpose for living.

"Hey Aunt Sarah! I just wanted you to know that I hosted a bowling tournament last week. It reminded me of the time you and I arranged a mini-golf tournament at work. It was fun. Love, Adam"

Adam, so funny and playful and big hearted. Very few of us knew he had a melancholy side, but then who doesn't? The potential is in any one of us to at some point lose our sense of grace and slip into the kind of despondent thinking that hides in the shadows. Hopefully we move quickly out of it so there's no chance we would be caught there entertaining thoughts that we would outright deny if they were brought into the light.

We would rather fake it and say, "I'm fine!" than say how we really feel. If he would have just talked about it. Keeping the despair inside made it grow bigger until all perspective was lost. How can a funny and handsome guy get to the place where he believed he was going nowhere? Almost 35 years old and having nothing in life, traveling on a path he didn't even like? It's the place where desperation totally outmaneuvers common sense. The place where one starts to think the only way out is to end it all. The place where one says it once, then twice, then again…"I'll just shoot myself."

No one knew that he was even thinking about actually making a plan to use his gun, on himself. Apparently he thought by doing that his agony would be ended, never thinking it would instead create the beginning of what seemed like endless and relentless pain for so many others, especially his mom, Joan.

I didn't know his mom but I learned that she was coming in for a Reiki treatment. I was told that she had lost her son through suicide and could I help. The night before she was scheduled to come in, I was prayerfully sending Reiki ahead of time to the session when the idea came to me that I could send Reiki to Adam. Send Reiki to Adam, really? I had never heard of giving Reiki to someone who had died. How would that work?

Would a soul who had already crossed over even need Reiki? The thought persisted so I agreed. All right, I'll send him Reiki. I quieted myself, invited his presence, and listened.

That was first time I had met Adam. The image of him that I saw showed his head bowed low between his knees. He couldn't lift his head up, and he looked as if he honestly didn't have the will to even try. I could feel sorrow and shame, his entire countenance pulled under by the weight of it. The energy around him felt like confusion, shock, and disbelief. The feelings were like it might feel if you thought you made the biggest mistake ever and were not able to ever fix it, like there was no turning back. It felt like equally there was no moving forward either.

He looked like a soul trapped in despair, not looking up enough to see the gentle and loving crowd of spirits around him. I could see on their spirit faces and feel from their essence that there was no judgment from these witnesses, only caring and compassion. I wanted to reach out and lift up Adam's head so he could see them, but I knew this was something he would have to do on his own, in his own time.

As I watched the scene, I continued sending Reiki and love energy. I could feel the tingling sensation in my hands grow stronger, and the resonance in the energy flow became more powerful. The Reiki began moving so quickly and deeply that my hands were literally shaking and moving on their own accord. The vibrational intensity didn't let up for what seemed like a long time, yet my hands never tired from reaching towards Adam. Soon, Source gave the word that it was enough, for now.

My hands and arms stopped moving, and I lowered them while still feeling waves of love and healing light flowing to Adam. I sat quietly for a time, thinking about Adam, innately knowing that the mist of love and healing surrounding him would continue to minister to his aching heart. Finally I drifted off to sleep.

The next morning when I woke up, I immediately thought of Adam. I began sending Reiki, and again the intensity of it made my hands and arms move back and forth. Feeling all that resonance, I knew the Reiki energy was flowing from one dimension to another touching him right where he was. I don't have any idea how that could literally happen or be explained. But why not? Vibration is vibration.

I might have questioned the validity of it all had it not been happening to me. To experience it and feel the power of it made it real and humbling, to say the least. The important question was could it help Adam? I felt a compassionate love for him and a wish for his healing so that he could once again lift his head and his soul.

Later that day Adam's mom came in for the Reiki treatment. My heart ached for her as my own motherly instincts kicked in. How devastating and heart-breaking to lose a son to suicide. All the "if only's" that must be plaguing her thoughts. If only she had known he was hurting so badly. If only she had come home 5 minutes earlier that day. If only she had returned his call sooner. We persecute ourselves with all the torturing we do when someone has taken themselves away from us, feeling like we could have stopped them, should have stopped them, and feeling like it must have somehow been our fault.

I know Reiki energy has amazing healing power, and I trusted that the energy flow would help this lovely woman find peace and healing. I heard myself asking for divine guidance and for as many ascended masters as possible to be with us. I quietly lifted Joan's treatment agenda to the Divine.

As I meditated, I recognized a presence of energy. It was Adam coming to the forefront. I recognized his spirit. "Adam, how are you doing? Welcome! You know your mom is here. She loves you so much. Is there anything you'd like to say to her?"

Just as I had seen him last night and this morning, his head was between his knees prostrated in despair. He wanted to acknowledge his mom, but he just couldn't face her. He knew how much pain he had caused her and for what? Some stupid thought he had been thinking about how his life sucked? Some stupid thing about how manly it was and vigilante-like to take things into his own hands? And now, oh now.

Just as I was wondering what I could possibly do or say, Freddy appeared. Freddy is a spirit soul I had met some time ago through another client. He had shot himself and died by suicide a couple of years ago. Freddy came right over to Adam and stood by him. He said, *"Adam, I'm here for you. I know what you're feeling, and I'm going to help you. I'm going to show you all kinds of things about your new digs here. Trust me, you can do this. You can get through this."*

I knew that Adam was in good hands with Freddy. While they connected, I continued the Reiki with his mom. When it felt right, I began to share with her what I had seen, felt, and heard. She said she too felt Adam's presence! She had been quietly talking to him.

And yes, she knew Freddy. She smiled and said, "That sounds just like Freddy. I am so glad he is there with Adam." Joan seemed relieved. We finished our Reiki session and she looked brighter and less dazed for having had a chance to feel a connection to Adam. She closed with what I would hear many more times to come, "I love and like you Adam, you know I always will."

There were more Reiki treatments for Joan and consistent visits from Adam. As you can imagine, overcoming the grief was very difficult for Joan. She expressed at times that she had lost her own will to live.

She felt like she had nothing left to live for as depression set in deeply. Spirit said to her: *"Who are you? You are Light. That's enough. You are enough. Your presence is enough. Eventually you will awaken to a purpose for living rather than a reason for dying."* The words were so healing, and the love of Spirit was so present.

And Adam? Over time he gradually lifted his head up. He finally was able to look at his mom and his sister and communicate his love to them. Joan was able to ask and learn that he was OK, that yes he knew his sister had moved, and yes he saw the goings on of the family. What does he do all day? He zips here and there, spends time learning and visiting, working on his issues, and oh by the way, Grandpa George is with him whenever he wants him there and, *"he's as funny as ever, sometimes telling the same ole' jokes."*

Adam was in a place of unconditional love, and I could see that he was healing. From his expression and his energy, I sensed that he accepted the love all around him and was finally able to forgive himself. He began to look wide-eyed and strong, healthy and confident. He took an interest in the family he left behind and learned from Freddy funny ways to make his Spirit presence known. He blew out candles, knocked over pictures, and interrupted TV shows. His mom was grateful for all of it. She always expressed her continuing love for him.

Later, Joan became sick with cancer. Adam had strong words of advice and directives expressing his love for her and his strong wish that she take care of herself. He told her with conviction, *"It is not your time yet to be with me! You have so many more things to do on earth. You gotta stay there and keep loving all those grandkids. Do what you do best which is to take them places, have them over, make cookies. Make memories with them."*

Strongest of all was another mission he gave to his mom. Insistent that she do it, he spoke in a confident and loud voice, *"Tell everyone that suicide is not an option. Tell them don't even think about it!"*

Joan is now working tirelessly to share the message and has done so in creative ways. Adam told her she could reach kids by raising money to build a fence for creating a safe playground. Over time she could add play equipment to the playground in his memory. She could use those opportunities to encourage kids to talk about what's on their minds and to support kids to play, interact, and make friends so that no one ever feels so alone that they want to die.

Adam knew his mom needed money to help in the effort so he suggested she do fundraisers and create a "Sports R Us" fund. He suggested having fishing contests to raise awareness and have people donate money through a contest fee. This was a perfect project because he loved fishing. One of the last photos taken of Adam shows him standing proudly holding a large fish he had caught.

For another project, he suggested having yard sales. He said, *"Tell people to donate stuff they don't want anymore. Keep things only if they make you happy. Keeping extra stuff is not about someday maybe I'll use that as much as does it make me happy right now?"*

It worked. Joan raised enough money to build the fence around the playground and more. Getting involved in the efforts has had a positive healing effect for her *and* has helped many kids. Wonderful.

Joan continued Reiki treatments, and once asked, "Do I have angels around me?"

Archangel Michael came through and said, *"We are always around you. We know you still feel sadness, and you will. Try this. Imagine putting the sadness in a box, especially when it feels over-whelming. Tuck it in then give it up to me. I will lift it up to the Light and Love of God where the sad energy will be changed and returned to you as love energy to love yourself and others. Then, when you can, do things that you find joy in to replace the sadness. It's OK to take just one step at a time."*

SPIRIT SPEAKS: *You are Light. That's enough. You are enough. Your presence is enough.*

SPIRIT SPOTLIGHT: Suicide

What can we all learn from this true story? For one thing, we can focus on developing coping skills. Learning ways to manage life in our ever-changing world of stressors can be taught from a very young age and on up. There are many ways to cope starting with learning to experience and accept ourselves as spiritual beings. Even children can learn how to invite Spirit to be a part of their lives as they see it modeled by parents, caretakers and other adults in their world.

As we grow and our problems become more complicated, there are more coping skills to learn to help us work through the regrets from perceived mistakes, the discouragement and pain from challenges and upheaval, and the difficult emotions from losing a loved one. There are many steps to the processes, and we will each have our own way that works best.

We can focus on our choices of how we are going to think about and relate to others. We can intentionally work to be more understanding. That leads to more compassion and cooperation.

We can practice not judging others, including anyone taking their own life. The only soul judging Adam for choosing to take his own life was Adam himself. He brought his journey with him to the Other Side, and while not escaping the need to face things head on, he did get a pass on negative criticism from the souls around him. From the moment he crossed over, the community of Spirit was supportive and loving. The unconditional compassion and acceptance helped him in resolving his issues and healing his soul. Those same welcoming qualities help anyone of any age in any situation to cope, pick up their spirit, and thrive.

It may take learning, practice, experience, inspiration, and asking Spirit for help to develop those qualities. We can start with intention now to choose thoughts and actions that take us to acceptance and grace. This intentional awareness of others will be the pre-emptive step to minimizing the choices that lead to despair and what ultimately may take one to the place of taking their own life.

On the other side, Adam is experiencing the sacredness of unconditional love. We, too, can receive it from Spirit on this side where we are. Spirit is just as supportive of us here as of souls on the other side.

What helped both Adam and his mom lift their heads up again? She connected with Spirit, realized that souls live on, and sent continuing love through the veil. Adam connected with Spirit, lifted his head to see the loving souls around him, and received healing. For both of them, letting go of the painful parts became easier as they discovered and received love and healing energy from Spirit. We can do the same.

The healing energy of the mother and son's love and respect for each other crossed through the dimensions both ways. Adam focused on helping Joan with a project, she put her energies into loving him and carrying out the project. There was healing on both sides of the veil. They both attended to their spirit side while they both attended to healing from grief. It is spiritual work with the promise of better days ahead.

Attend to your spirit at least as much as your schedule.
With that, you have a better chance of balancing your life.
Balance in life could prevent the need to end it.

Where's Betty?

Divert the energy of fear about the changes and finalities of old age into noticing instead this very moment.

One of my favorite senior citizens came in for Reiki. It was her birthday, and the treatment was a gift from her daughter. Helene is one of those vibrant seniors ready to keep up with the latest except she doesn't eat Kale no matter how trendy or healthy. She says she prefers to cook it in lots of olive oil so it will slip easier into the garbage bin as she grabs the potato chip bag instead.

Helene's daughter was there in the room with us and it was wonderful to all be together for the Reiki. Having invited and called upon the help of our team of spirit healers, we settled into the quiet moments of the calming Reiki. I gently looked up after a time, and there, at Helene's crown chakra, appeared an enthusiastic group of spirits who were smiling and anxious to tell me about who they were. They said, *"Helene has been collecting and building up this team over the years. We're her crew!"*

I thanked them and focused on co-creating with them the continuing healing experience for Helene. The energy felt like, if you can imagine, a rolling in of holiness and sanctity. I bowed in silence as the energy pulsed around us.

My mind then went strangely to thoughts about aging and how our aging brings its own set of challenges, the dwindling of our family and friends as people and pets keep dying around us, the reminder of our human fragility as our body parts slow down, and then there's that potential of losing our independence or losing our mind at some point down the road. I wondered if that is something that Helene has been worried about.

I asked Spirit, "How are we to cope with aging? It's terrible to imagine myself slipping into senility and, what the heck? We have this fruitful, adventurous life, then it comes to this?"

Dear Sharyn, Helene too is asking the same questions. Here is what can help: Live in this present moment. Divert the energy of fear about the difficult changes and the scary finalities of old age into noticing instead **this very moment.** *And notice that this very present moment is what we all have for* <u>every</u> *moment of our human life experience, and it continues on eternally as the only "time" factor that there is in the spirit realm.*

There is no other "time" on the other side, as the concept of time is a human thing. There is, however, the present moment. Living in the moment—not multitasking, not thinking ahead, not remembering the past, not rushing, not worrying, not pressuring yourself to complete a task—is more powerful than what you can imagine. There is more to experience in the practice of living in the present moment. You can practice this here on the earth plane, and you will continue with the practice on the other side.

Divert the energy of fear and become stronger by noticing the present moment. In so doing appreciate all the beloved details of your life, all the perfect manifestations of your desires, and all the potential that surrounds you, in peace. You will be inspired to let go of the efforts of concern or worry and instead put your efforts into things that have eternal value.

This is what has eternal value: the Universal Laws of Love, Oneness, Free Will, Manifestation, Compassion, Mercy. Add 'This Present Moment,' a Universal Law for every living being.

You have seen Helene's spirit team with her. Know that this team and spirit connection is on the eternal list as well, so add that to what has eternal value. The presence of spirit, communication with spirit, and the spirit team chosen by and for every living being will always be available now and forever.

Think on those things. But of course, as the saying goes, don't ever become so heavenly minded that you are no earthly good. No need to be eternally minded at all costs. Enjoy your life and all the earthly pleasures that are part of it. Simply remember, particularly when life is challenging, that there is wisdom and healing from noticing the present moment. It will lift you from a path of descending to a path of ascension.

Thankful for the quietness of the sacred space of the Reiki, I enjoyed the brilliant, flowing colors of the healing energies, the purples and greens, and the lightness of the air. Unexpectedly, Helene's dog, Rusty, jumped in. Rusty is a senior citizen dog that Helene recently adopted from an owner who had to move into a nursing home. Helene says he has a split personality and sometimes wants to be called Bernard.

So Rusty jumped in and asked me to tell Helene, *"Thank you so much for accepting me for who I am even though it's crazy sometimes. And I want you to know that I'm just like you because neither of us is 'rusty.' We're not old and cranky and rusty. We have a lot more life to give!"*

Too funny, that Rusty humor. With a sigh and a namaste of gratitude, I knew the session was winding down. I gently checked in to see how Helene was doing, and she opened her eyes with a burst of excitement wanting to talk about what she had seen and felt. "The variations of the yellow I saw were just indescribable. Stunning!"

We shared the messages and insights, and finally I asked Helene if she had any other questions. "Yes, yes," she said. She became quite somber and asked, "Where's Betty? We all want to know where she is. We feel other people around us but where's Betty?"

I asked, "Who is Betty? Has Betty passed?"

"Yes, Betty has passed. She's my mother." The more we talked, the more Helene sounded agitated and anxious to know what was up. "Nobody has heard from her or felt her energy or sensed her presence for a long, long time."

It only took a moment, and there was the spirit of Betty. I could hear her say, "I've been on retreat." It didn't sound like a happy retreat as I could detect her estranged feelings and see her posture of solemnity and shoulders drooped. Betty continued saying that nobody had heard from her since she died because she was on retreat to deal with some things. I asked her what was she dealing with, how it was going, and... my own tears began to flow as I could feel her feelings of guilt and despair.

Betty said, talking directly to Helene, while I channeled for her, "You can't feel my presence because I can't face anyone. I'm so ashamed. I don't know how you could ever forgive me. My behavior was not really who I am. Please hear me: My behavior was not who I am. I behaved terribly and please, if I could have just..."

I looked over at Helene and her daughter and could see that they both had tears streaming down their cheeks. We all were crying as we listened and felt the energy of her confession. I know from chatting with other souls who have crossed that going to heaven may mean the body is healed because we no longer have its physical limitations, the blind can see and the lame can walk. But going to heaven doesn't mean the personality suddenly jumps to sainthood or that the mind and soul automatically heals from its wounds.

Here was Betty, aware in the new Light that her behavior was not what she wished it had been. I don't know what the back story is, but I could feel the deep sense of shame, sorrow, and regret. In this moment of Betty's vulnerability, I could see on the faces of Helene and her daughter that something was resonating deeply. Betty continued through her own broken hearted tears, "Please forgive me. Please forgive me."

I shared with Helene and her daughter what Betty was saying and feeling, and I also shared what I had learned from chatting with the dead. "As souls on the other side," I said, "we have opportunities to heal. Surrounded by the unconditional love of our spirit team there we can forgive ourselves, we can change, evolve, and eventually grow into embracing new purpose. We can learn how to help those we have left behind on the earth plane."

"Equally," I continued, "those of us still here on the earth can help souls who have crossed over by praying for them and sending them Reiki and healing energy. It would mean a lot to Betty if you could find it in your heart to send her love and forgive her."

I left that for them to decide while I offered healing energy for them all. I thanked Betty for coming to us. Turning to Helene and her daughter, I invited them to sit quietly for a few moments and take in the presence of spirit. I could sense a softening of their feelings, and it felt like resolution was in the air.

SPIRIT SPEAKS: *Noticing the present moment...you will be inspired to let go of the efforts of concern or worry and instead put your efforts into things that have eternal value.*

SPIRIT SPOTLIGHT: This Present Moment

Interestingly, after Helene told me that no one had heard from Betty for a long, long time, it took only a quick moment for Betty's soul to speak up. There it is again, the moment, taking a moment, being in the moment, speaking up in a moment, and seeing in a moment. It just took a moment of conversation for new understanding to erase Helene's fears and frustrations about her mom's lack of connection. What could "being in the moment" look like if I applied it in my life? How could it guide my understanding of how to help the elderly, be a better caretaker, and how to soothe my own concerns about getting old?

Let's try what Spirit said. Let's try guiding the seniors and us back to "the present moment." It would distract them from fear, from thinking about the scary unknowns, and from feeling so much loss. They could go from missing what they don't have anymore to focusing on what they do have which is **this moment**.

It powerfully takes us into their world to join them in their moment which may be a world where sound is muffled, the physical body hurts, making decisions is confusing, and all the activity feels like a bustling overwhelm that is neither familiar nor inviting. It would bring us all to the moment where life really is meaningful because we are doing, feeling, expressing, noticing, and having purpose in that moment. That is the reason for living rather than dying.

Can we ever embrace the power of seizing the present moment? What if we could stop the multi-tasking and instead smell the fragrance of a precious connection, a revitalized noticing of what we never saw before, a refreshing breath coming through the heart?

Staying in the moment is like the power of a photograph to stop the action of nature so we can notice things we had never seen before like the spikes on the soft Lamb's Ear, the moon-like landscape of the core of the petunia, the fur coat vest on the back of a bee, or the straw from the mouth of the butterfly.

I could feel the gratitude and thanks pouring out of me for all we have and for all the more we can discover that we have by simply noticing the present moment. We have a breath that brings life, we have a heart that brings connection, and we have a celestial team patiently wanting to be invited into the moment. I wonder what else we might notice when we stop to be present.

Spirit points out that more than a cliché or pat answer, 'This Present Moment' has an effect to not only lift us out of fear and take us to a better emotional place, but it also has an eternal element. It's right up there with the other contemplations of growing old that prompt us to realize that it does us well to spend time and energy on things, concepts, actions that have <u>eternal value</u>.

Like Spirit suggested, we can divert the energy leak of fear and instead, in peace, become stronger by noticing the beloved details of life, the perfect manifestations, and the potentials all around us. We will have more energy to put into the things that have eternal value. What has eternal value?

Spirit says, for one thing, the Universal Laws have eternal value. They are: *Love, Oneness, Free Will, Manifestation, Compassion, and Mercy.* They will exist eternally as principles that govern everything in the Universe and are essential for balance and harmony. Spirit added to the list "this present moment." , and our spirit team have eternal value.

Also of eternal value are people, their soul, and our soul with all its memories, experiences, and evolutions. Practical application?

Every time we prioritize our day, then we are practicing staying in the moment and keeping eternity's values in view. As my friend Sylvia says, imagine you have five gold coins of energy given to you every morning. How will you spend your coins today? How will you prioritize your time, efforts, love, and your moments?

Every time we give our time and effort to the benefit of grounding and strengthening our soul, and every time we feed our soul with meditation, prayer, devotions, sacred text reading, then we are practicing staying in the moment and keeping eternity's values in view.

Every time we offer the sacrifices of service and we offer Soul Service using our spiritual gifts like hospitality, giving, teaching, and loving, then we are practicing staying in the moment and keeping eternity's values in view.

Every time in relationships when we choose to go the path of love instead of reactive defense, every time we reach for gratitude instead of complaints, and every time we bite our tongue instead of indulging in negative conversation, then we are practicing staying in the moment and keeping eternity's values in view.

Every time we work our job soulfully, honestly, with diligence and commitment, then we are practicing staying in the moment and keeping eternity's values in view.

Every time we notice and discipline ourselves about what we take in whether through our eyes, ears, or mouth, and every time we stop the loop of our negative thinking by choosing a higher thought, then we are practicing staying in the moment and keeping eternity's values in view.

Eventually we will know the ease of experience when time seems to have no relevance because each moment is spent — in the moment. There are some things we can hold on to forever, and there are some things we cannot hold on to at all.

> He is no fool who gives up what he cannot keep
> to gain that which he cannot lose.   Jim Elliott

I AM the Rainbow
...as if dying means losing all that you gained by living.
What if dying is less about an end and
more about a transition?

When I met the spirit of this beloved Greek mother and grandmother, I could tell she loved going for the best of all there is. She radiated zest for life even from the other side. Her daughters said that Mama Bresia's gusto never wavered throughout her life of more than nine decades. All the knitting, sewing, decorating, organizing, cooking, baking, traveling... talk about a lesson in keeping active. Her motto was, "Be of service, try new things, and stay forever young at heart." She was as happy in Prescott, NY, as she was in her birthplace in Athens, Greece, as long as she could get her Chai Lattes at the Try-A-Cup tea house.

One of Bresia's daughters, Kalli, is a published poet and friend of mine. I had just read her email about her mother's passing before going to bed, so I started praying for the family. I had no idea that Bresia in spirit would stop by. I was about to turn out the light when I heard as clear as a bell, *"Get a tablet with lots of paper on it. I have lots to say."* So I did, and here is the message:

To my family, *I know it's hard to have an empty space where I was. I would fill it for you if I could. But that's not the way of life. We have to experience these empty places sometimes.*

I wish I could show you the way of Spirit because that is the way of life that goes on much longer than the earthly physical life, forever in fact. Maybe there are moments when the way of Spirit feels familiar to you because it is. Yet most of the time when talking about it on the earth plane, Spirit talk can sound like gibberish because it's so esoteric. It's so out there.

Bring it in to your heart. The best way to be in touch with the way of Spirit is through the blending of your mind and heart. You are doing it when you miss me. The memories are in your mind, the sadness is in your heart. Together they are in a dimension that's closest to where I am.

Earth is where you are. You are on your journey, and a great journey it is. I love that I can still be a part of that journey in my spirit form. I am with you in a different way now but with the same love.

I hear the question, "What is the purpose of living if we end up dying?" as if dying means losing all that you gained by living. What if dying is less about an END and more about a TRANSITION?

Consider dying as a transition, and transition is inevitable. Like a butterfly transitioning from a cocoon. Understanding it for what it is helps in the acceptance of it. It's a shifting, a passing through one dimension to another. Death isn't the end of the soul, it's just a change. It's the end of the physical body because that does not pass through, but the soul passes through.

You don't need to be looking or longing for this soul passage right now because you are still in the earth life. Be happy in it, it'll be over soon enough. Don't wish away any opportunity to elevate consciousness which is the learning that earth living gives, a developing of your own consciousness and a growing of the consciousness of the entire planet.

How can you get through missing me? How can anyone get through the grief of loss? Asking the questions about death and dying is fine. The seeking is worthwhile. The finding is glorious. Then finally, accepting of transition is one big step forward for the ascension of the soul. Ask, seek, find, and accept.

When your cousin died you were so sad. In those times, and when the children you work with are struck with emotions about death and loss, and when you are touched by and traumatized by your grief or theirs, it is all a step of ascension. There is dying and grief, and then comes meaning and ascension. Experiencing death is difficult, certainly not fun, until you get to the Other Side.

From here where I am, it all makes sense. Trust the process of dying like you trust the process of writing. You teach children to write because the process of it is so wonderful for their soul. Likewise, trust the process of transition. The course of life was created with birth and death, with beginnings and endings for good reason. Being on the earth plane then transitioning when we die is all part of a process that you can trust.

I can tell you that it is worth going through. The going through is really a "Coming Home," a coming to the pure spirit dimension, and a coming to the place of letting go of human limitations. Imagine that.

Writing too is a letting go. Writing frees the mind and frees the soul from its limitations. Then at some point you realize that in that freedom, sometimes there are no words to describe a feeling like the depth of sadness or the height of joy. At that point, you are in the vicinity of understanding there is more. There are more dimensions outside of the human body. There is soul-ness, consciousness, and spirit. Trust that the process will lead you there.

Enough about grief. None of us likes that part of life until, like I said, you get to the Other Side. Then you get to see the bigger picture.

I am fine. I am ascending. I am flying. I am loving you. I am with the family. I am with all our loved ones. I am living in unconditional love.

Multiply the beauty and wonder of creation a hundred fold and that's where I am. I am with the angels. I am with God. I am jumping over, I am sliding down, I am absorbing the delight of the Rainbow Bridge we so often talked about. In fact, I AM the rainbow. This is what I want you to know.

Yes, I miss being with you in person. I am also delighting in being your Spirit Guardian. Son of a gun, I get to be your Angel. I get to show you the colors of the rainbow.

I love you, Mom

SPIRIT SPEAKS: *From here where I am, it all makes sense.*

SPIRIT SPOTLIGHT: Transition

There are times when I want to reject the death part of life because it's too darn hard. But, I understand more about it now, and it helps to see it not as an end to be feared or overcome, but rather a transition to recognize and accept for its benefits. Like Mama Bresia said, it is coming to a place where there are no earthly limitations, where we get to fly and soar.

There are universal reasons why we all have to go through the dying process. The limits of being human, including the limits of aging, are with purpose. We come here by design, with God's oversight and with the vision and cooperation of a team of Angels and Guides, to learn what we want to learn, to gift our soul with experiencing limits and growing from it. We take that with us when we die. Not pockets full of things, not houses, money, or cars, but we take our memories, lessons learned, our expanded soul and all that it has evolved to be. Would our daily life look any different if we believed that? Our schedule would, and our list of worries and fears would.

I love Mama Bresia's reminder to trust the process. That could be the word of the day, trust. And I love saying out-loud, "I AM the rainbow!" Try saying it out-loud. It's fun! Kalli told me that her mom always felt a guardian angel was beside her while she was alive, and she imagined death as a journey to the end of the rainbow. How great that after riding the rainbow arch, she found not a rainbow's end but rather the I AM.

Know that we are all with you, loving you, and watching
over you. We will be laughing the loudest
as you entertain others.

You will be able to do that again. And you will do it
honestly with real joy and laughter from your heart.

Watch for me! I exist beyond all limitations.

PART II
HOW TO CONNECT

SECTION V: HOW TO CONNECT WITH SPIRIT

Connecting with Spirit is an outcome of who we are by birthright, who we've become by the choices we've made in our lives, and who we want to be by intention.

Communication With Spirit

It may seem radical to connect with Spirit until you remember that it has been going on for a long, long time. People have been praying for centuries, talking to their God, asking, receiving, thanking, and crediting God for divine interventions and inspirations. If moving beyond these fundamentals seems like woo woo, your concerns can be soothed with the understanding and experience of it.

To speak with Spirit and hear the unique perspective of our Loved Ones, Angels, God, and other Beings of Light makes it worthwhile to learn how to connect. The communication offers what we are all meant to receive—Spirit messages that are a reliable resource of wisdom, love, and guidance to support our earth journey.

How does it work? How can anyone hear messages from another dimension? What do we have to do? Read the lists of ideas, tools to use, and steps to connect to help it happen. Communication can be as simple as wanting to connect, getting quiet, and listening respectfully for the conversation. Done. Or it can be as multi-layered and diverse as there are beings in our multiverse.

The multitude of ideas are not meant to overwhelm but simply to inform you about what is out there to work with. Choose what works for you and you'll talk with Spirit in a more profound way than you ever knew was possible.

Sometimes it happens because we are ready and waiting. Sometimes it's simply a Gift. There is a learning curve and over time, with practice, it gets easier. It is available to every soul. It may feel challenging because challenges are part of our journey, but you are never out of reach of connection with Spirit.

Who Spirit Is

When we talk about messages from Spirit, it is natural to ask, "Who is Spirit?" The most recognizable definition of Spirit is "creative energy" or Creator, often stated as the Source of All That Is. The single identity of Spirit found in all major religions is God who goes by other names as well such as Jehovah, Allah, YHWH, Yahweh, El Shaddai, and the Almighty.

Spirit, however, also refers to the God energy that goes by different identities according to history, culture, geography, religion, beliefs, and lifestyle. Spirit is a collective of identities, any of who could show up with powerful messages for guidance and healing. It is the flexibility, genius, and unconditional love of God the Creator to offer such a variety of identities to meet the needs of the diversity of humanity.

Spirit could be any of the ascended masters who have been recognized, worshipped and adored for centuries such as Jesus, the Holy Spirit, Gautama Buddha, Mother Mary, Isis, Djwal Khul, Melchizedek or Goddess Quan Yin. Spirit could be deceased loved ones, departed pets, animal totems, guardians, Reiki guides, spirit guides, angels, and archangels. Spirit can be your own higher self. Spirit can be groups of beings such as the Collective or Matrix Masters or cosmic and galactic groups such as the Arcturians and Pleiadians. Spirit can be all of the above making one grand Ocean of Love.

One of the great benefits for me as a practitioner is that I get to meet the variety. I have met the personalities of many of the above, and I know for certain that Spirit will graciously show up as the one identity that a person needs at any moment in time, appearing in the form they will recognize and can most easily connect to.

Look for the variety of them in the true **Spirit Speaks** stories and see the evidence in the confirmations. Look at your own stories and your own confirmations. Spirit's revelations of who they are will come to you personally. The evidence is in the resonance you feel, the truths that speak to your knowing, and in what you seek for and then find, like gold nuggets of wisdom just for you.

The evidence that I've seen reveals Spirit to be, whether singular or plural, remarkable beings who patiently and graciously relate to us with an astounding unconditional love that leads, guides, accepts, and comforts. They understand our soul history, our wounding, and our survivals. They know our need for strength, happiness, clarity, and relationships. They get it that we need them and can use their gifts of synchronicities, miracles, and personal touches. It's all true. I've seen them at work.

This is what they have to say about who they are:
As part of the Other Side, We are Spirit with Universal Wisdom, Light, and Love. We are versions of the collective consciousness of humanity and are available for you to access for Universal Wisdom, Light, and Love. We, Spirit, are available and want to be of service.

How Spirit Reveals Itself

I love the stories of how Spirit comes through. There are signs, synchronicities, songs, a still small voice as subtle as a gentle breeze or a voice as tangible as a boot in the keister. You may have received a message last night in a dream, or maybe today you got a message as a flash of insight or twinge of consciousness. Have you ever been awed by being in the right place at the right time having been nudged there by an inner knowing? How about the many angel stories and the testimonies that leave us saying, "You just can't make this up."

Spirit once revealed itself to me as an angel who was as human as any angel I've ever seen. In her big, black minivan she pulled over and rescued my young son and me after my car broke down in the middle of winter along a major highway to Syracuse. She called for a tow truck on her car phone, which at the time was a cutting-edge innovation; in fact, I didn't even know anyone who owned a car phone.

Then she drove us ten miles to the school where I was a teacher and my son a first grader. She saved my day and was now my new favorite human on the planet. The next day I mailed her a heart-felt thank you using the address on the business card she gave me. Three days later, the letter came back as undeliverable. "No such addressee." Really? One of those angels disguised as human, no doubt.

Spirit reveals itself in other clever ways. My deceased brother-in-law showed up while we were at Disney with some Goofy Dust of his own. There we were in the family suite munching goodies when I decided to turn on the TV. I sat down in front of it and the darn thing, by itself, switched off. Who sat on the remote? Where IS the remote? Never mind, the TV came back on. Then off. Then on. Then off. "Dick, is that you?"

"Yes it is. This is fun manipulating the TV. Just wanted to let you know I'm with you even at Disney! Have Fun Y'all."

Fun and fulfilling revelations of Spirit can be in the coincidences like when my brother, an avid Steeler's football fan, and my sister-in-law were driving to a friend's house and they made a wrong turn. That activated a re-calculating of the GPS that took them so far off base that they had to stop for gas and, of course, used the pump that wouldn't accept their credit card. So they had to pay inside which is where it was, the exact Steeler's pin that they had been looking for for over two years! Was that Spirit giving them a blessing? The ways Spirit reveals itself are endlessly personal and creative.

Spirit may appear as an identity we recognize, or Spirit may appear as energy. Spirit may come as a flash of light, as balls of fire, or a kaleidoscope of colors. You may feel the personality of Spirit, the peace of their presence or the heat of their high frequency. Once again, the appearance is diverse yet still the same Spirit, the same essence.

Experiencing that essence, connecting with Spirit, regardless of the identity for form, gives us a chance to experience other dimensions, and encounter the infinite. Spirit models variety and connection for us so we can better understand Oneness and Unconditional Love.

Some revelations of Spirit are less fundamental than light, peace, or synchronicities such as when Spirit speaks up as a voice during a Reiki treatment, or appears as a Native American chief during a meditation, or through tools like oracle cards or rune stones. You might find yourself journaling conversations with words and thoughts that you know are not your own. Spirit reveals itself in countless ways yet always personal and on target.

How It Happened For Me

Maybe it was the desire in my heart that led me to be in the vicinity of hearing Spirit, maybe it was my constant seeking which in turn manifested choices and intentions that led me to talking with Spirit. Maybe it was those tough childhood traumas that took me to a deep place for survival.

Maybe it was my sanctuary of the church, my interest in going to Bible college where I kept running into sacred texts to study and mentors to learn from who knew how to connect with Spirit. Maybe it was just meant to be.

Thankfully, people showed up who taught me Reiki and helped me understand energy work, healing, and transformation. From there, I experienced a whole new relationship with Spirit. Reiki was to become my connection tool for even more of Spirit.

One day when I was giving a Reiki treatment, I heard a voice in my head as clear as a bell. *"Spend time giving Reiki to her 5th chakra and then ask her what truth is she not able to verbalize."* What? *"And then tell her that her chronic foot problem will clear up as soon as she decides to walk her own path instead of his."*

I knew I was hearing things but didn't really know at the time what was happening. I hesitated but decided to say what I heard out loud. That first time, and every time since then, Spirit brings messages that can be confirmed, that make sense, and are precisely correct for the healing it brings. The messages haven't stopped coming and the magnificence has never dulled.

Spirit wants all of humanity to, and I quote:
"Be in the Know, move beyond the fear of limiting beliefs, and move into a safe place to find your God-given holy resources. We are with you, invested in you, accessible and available to hear and answer your questions, and eager to help you manifest your best life ever."

How It Works
The fact that it happens is why I share the stories, along with the fact that messages come in such glory and truth. I've seen it, heard it, and felt the awe. I ask you to consider the evidence, listen to your own resonance, and choose steps to help you hear and receive your own messages. Communication with Spirit is not something you need to be certified to do, it is not about projecting your own feelings or thoughts, it is not guessing what other dimensions expect us to say or be, and it is not setting up a presumption of what Spirit will offer. It is transformative, it exists, and there are steps to help it happen

How does it work? Although spirit communication is not an exact science, it is scientific. Begin the pursuit and you will find more than you expect of documented research and scrutiny. Scientists and researchers have studied telecommunications over the years, the anatomy of communication, the physics of vibration, and how to build a receiver.

Quantum physics is filling in the blanks about our DNA and how we are wired for this, about energy, and about our extended Universes otherwise called the Multiverse. There is more science now than ever about telepathy, mediumship, prayer, and near-death experiences. Look up Brain to Brain Interface or Synaptic Transference which is basically the study of the science of vibration, energy, and telepathy, all which are involved in communication with Spirit. Fundamental physics, quantum physics, and insights about DNA are all related to the big questions and the vocabulary of resonance, encoding, entrainment, strings, and strands. Google it.

Science has not yet built a device to communicate with Spirit or other dimensions, but here's the good news. We are the device. We are the sender, the receiver, the translator, the tower, and the satellite. If you find yourself feeling discouraged because you perceive you weren't born psychic or extraordinary, the fact is you were born with the ability to have heightened perceptions and to communicate with Spirit. Even if you don't feel as clued in as someone else, simply decide to join them, because you can! We all possess the ability to communicate with Spirit as our God-given birthright.

Spirit communication is about YOU strengthening your perceptual modes and incorporating new levels of perception. It's YOU trusting your intuitive perception to the point of extraordinary. It's YOU having the intention to believe that there are Beings of Light who with their evolved perspective, omniscience, omnipresence and omnipotence, really want to communicate with us and have much to offer. Embrace how you are made, embrace the Gift.

Why communicate with Spirit?
Communicating with Spirit is healing on many levels, inspiring a doorway to understanding, to witnessing miracles, and to knowing

peace. The more you allow Spirit to help you and be expressed through you and through your psychic self, the more resources you have to give back to yourself, to others, and to your work. You become a person with amplified sensitivity learning more and more about your circuits, your psychic self, your potentials, and your purpose. You could become your own caller ID. You could be an animal communicator as well as a Spirit communicator. You could be a medium, a light worker, and co-creator for healing. It's your key to becoming extraordinary!

What Spirit Offers

Spirit's Mission Statement and Promise is this: Spirit is alive and well, available to help you, desiring to be of service, eager that everyone remember who they are, and wishing to acknowledge their joy in being part of your team. Spirit says: *"We are alive and well, and we are available to help you. We desire to be of service. We are eager to see you remember who you are. We are pleased to be part of your team."*

Take this journey. Communicate with your Spirit allies. Let yourself be a member of this magnificent partnership that I can't stop smiling about.

The benefits, the wonder, and the expansion are all worth the effort. What could possibly be more valuable than having the ear of your deceased loved one? Or the unconditional love and appreciation of your pet, to know they survived the transition, that they are happy? Or what could be more precious than the gaze of the Almighty? Or to receive guidance and love and to learn from Beings who have direct connection to God? Or to be guided by Spirit whose perspective covers the past and future with infinite knowledge in all directions of time and space? Infinite Intelligence has time for us. It is up to us to make the effort.

The *Spirit Speaks* stories are examples of what Spirit offers. I have seen healing start from the moment of hearing from Spirit. Hurting clients went on to become of great service when their grief became an inspiration to advocate for a cause or an avenue for positive change or a reason to love again. Like Spirit said in the story "Rock Bottom," *Communicating with the spirit of us is exactly where the source of miracles is found.*

Spirit has this magical way with their message that touches hearts with hope and Light. Spirit awakens your power. Spirit downloads answers, visions, and a-ha's that make you want to think differently, be more embracing of all living things, and let go of what you don't need. You have everything to gain by hearing what Spirit offers, and by trying it for yourself.

The How To Basics

Although different from normal conversations on the earth plane, spirit communication is not an experience you have to earn, the messages are not codes you have to decipher, or spoken in a language that you have to totally guess what they are trying to say. It's more about your wanting, asking, quieting, listening, and receiving.

The "how to" is basically this:

1. Quiet your mind. Invite Spirit to the conversation then listen, trust, allow, talk and hear.

2. Ask and watch for the signs, confirmations and the resonance.

3. Express your gratitude.

Much pre-paving is already done from the choices you have made and are making everyday particularly in regard to your beliefs and your state of being. By pre-paving I mean putting yourself in the vicinity of better connection. You can turn your dial to tune in more clearly every time you choose to take another step for developing your spirituality, intuition, imagination, and telepathy. That is another whole book. For now, simply your intentions and most assuredly your efforts to increase your chances of being receptive are rewarding.

Start with the basics. Remember: Spirit knows much and wants you to know. Spirit loves much and wants you to experience it. Spirit stands ready to communicate and wants you to be there.

How do I know it's them?

There are ways to know that the messages you hear are coming from Spirit and not your own thinking. You are not making it up. To ease the doubts, here are six tools to use:

1. **Notice the voice and tone.** As you grow to know yourself, your personality, and your tone, you will likewise get to know Spirit's voice, personality, and tone. There will be a difference between yours and theirs.

2. **Notice the message content.** When the message is information you didn't know, weren't even thinking about, or couldn't have ever come up with, you will know it is from Spirit.

3. **Notice how you feel about the message**. Does the message feel in alignment with what you already know about who Spirit is and who you are? Spirit's way feels gentle and comforting, and it resonates in its simple elegance. They never judge and never rush you. You will feel a smile inside, a resonance that will say, "This is right and true."

4. **Check in with your heart** for the status of your heart engagement. Draw your attention away from your mind down to your heart. Put your hand on your heart and notice how you are feeling or what your heart is saying. From there you will experience your clarity.

5. **You'll know because you'll be listening, not talking.** When your mind is quiet and still, you will receive. You will be aware of being receptive, not busy thinking or talking.

6. **You will know by the confirmations.** Can you feel or see the signs? If you don't, ask and watch for them. The phenomenon are not essential but are gifts when they come.

Spirit will never try to trick you. What they understand to be for your Highest Good is not a secret and it is not a guessing game. Practice getting to know them until you know that.

Don't worry that you will have a conversation with an evil spirit. The Power of Light will outshine darkness. Darkness cannot exist in the presence of Light. Trust in the Light of who you are and in the Love of Spirit. For discernment, use your perceptual modes and ask Spirit to protect you. Use the energy of crystals or other tools for cleansing any attachments or debris of lower energies that you feel have infected your aura or your energy anatomy. Most of all focus on loving and seeking the Light, and trusting Spirit. Stay in your high vibration and be the Light that always shines.

How do you know if the message is from Spirit?
- If the room feels bigger now because you have connected with something bigger
- If your space is quiet and the message is heard above all the noise around you
- If a message comes quickly, without hesitation
- If the message has clarity
- If the message feels sanctified and good
- If what you hear touches your soul
- If the message feels complete but focus is on your next best step rather than all the steps
- If you just know everything will be all right

Know your preferred perceptual modes because that's your preferred way of perceiving and Spirit just may start there in the communication. Perceptual modes are your five senses which, with practice and expansion, become the clairs that you have heard about: clairvoyance, clairaudience, clairsentience, claircognizance, clairgustance, clairsalience, clairempathy, and clairtangency.

We all have preferred ones that come across as our natural strengths and talents. Practice strengthening them by being on the lookout for opportunities to use them. Then work specifically with your sixth sense, that fabulous inner seeing, hearing, and knowing that goes beyond the ordinary. You will grow in confidence, and you will know it is Spirit. For practical ways to do this, look at the list of Communication Enhancers coming up.

Learning the Language

The language of Spirit is a language of vibrational frequency to be perceived, a language of the right brain. It may manifest as a gentle, quiet, invisible language that is more about feeling, sensing, and knowing than just speaking. Or the conversation may come across loudly with visible or audible words, objects, songs, pictures, visions or movies. You may sense an odd taste in your mouth or smell a scent that reminds you precisely of someone you know, and that starts the conversation. The doors are wide open for creativity in manifesting the conversation whether that sharing is about simple ideas, mystical impressions or complicated theories.

I have been asked, "Does Spirit speak in English?" Spirit does not need to choose a dialect because the dialect is vibration. When words are needed, you will interpret their vibration in the language that you understand.

What does the voice of Spirit sound like? You may experience it as sounding like your own voice. It may sound like the same inner voice as when you talk to yourself or the same inner voice as when you are praying. You are the device. Or it may have a unique sound of its own.

It's the personality of the voice that makes the difference, the intensity or velocity, or the feeling behind the message. Sometimes the frequency of the vibration makes the voice sound soprano which is how my little chihuahua sounds. Larger animals often have a deeper voice. The high frequency voice of Spirit comes across as an intensely high pitched buzzing in my ears. That's one of the signs that Spirit is present and has something to say. If the buzzing comes in the middle of the night, I pull out my journal and the voice goes from the buzzing to sounding like my own voice again as I journal.

Spirit language is multidimensional. Thank goodness because we are multi-dimensional. We get to use parts and expressions of who we are in ways we might not otherwise experience. As you develop those dimensional perceptions, you realize that what you are actually

experiencing is the magical language of telepathy. Telepathy is the language of spirit, the language of heaven.

It may come as a surprise but it makes perfect sense that the more you practice telepathy, the more sensitive you will become to the value of telepathic skills right here on the earth plane. Not only can you communicate with other dimensions, you can communicate with other species. Telepathy is the basis for communicating with animals, plants, our own body cells, and all living things. Telepathically we can communicate by means of energy through our perceptual senses by using words, pictures, and feelings. That is how we get from Bark to Hello. The steps to communicating with Spirit are the same steps for communicating with all living beings on the planet and beyond.

Be comfortable with "It's Not Happening Today."
What if nothing happens? That's a tough one, especially when we really, really want to talk to Spirit. If it's not happening, don't judge yourself or your efforts. Spirit is not judging you. You don't have to get it just right or be anything other than who you are. Just be present and allow the communication to happen in its own time. In the meantime, keep practicing and blooming. And relax.

The same is true for Spirit guidance. Maybe it's not happening today but it is cued up for tomorrow. Spirit has the timing right. Maybe it's other people or other things that need to come into alignment before your connection or guidance can come through or make sense. Believe and trust. You will be at the right place at the right time for your Highest Good.

When it doesn't happen, there may be blockers in your field. Take a look at the list of possibilities. To get to a more receptive state, you may be led to make changes like avoiding substances or chooses not to stay in an environment that dulls the mind or agitates it. No judgment, but there is room for thought and room for change if something different would be for your highest good.

If you don't notice a blocker, then go for more enhancers in your life. Your receptivity is strengthened by all your choices for what gives you healing, joy, and peace.

Communication Blockers
- Stress or fear
- Internal clutter or Monkey Mind
- External clutter and distractions
- Unbalanced diet like too much sugar, caffeine, or processed foods
- Heart issues like resistance, shields, masks, heart walls, barricades
- Trying too hard
- Notice your posture: Is it scrunched up, tense shoulders, and tight muscles?
- Being around people who ridicule you or do not believe you
- Overuse of substances such as drugs or alcohol

Communication Enhancers
- Revive gratitude by stating and feeling the positive.
- Cleanse and de-clutter by letting go of what no longer serves you.
- Use positive affirmations every day. Repeat your favorite mantras.
- Give it time.
- Ask for healing, seek healing on all levels including all your chakras.
- Ask for help to heal during your sleep when the mind is at rest.
- Accept the rest periods.
- Have a receptive posture: an open chest and listening pose.

- Adopt habits that reduce stress, and increase calmness.
- Use tools like Reiki or yoga, crystals or essential oils for healing and centering.
- Cut cords with anyone who has or may criticize or punish you.
- Play calming music. Move your body in dance.
- Improve your lifestyle with more rest, being outside, exercising, meditating, eating well.
- Let being in nature center you, awaken you with its beauty.

I asked Spirit for wisdom about what to do when it's not happening. This is what I heard:

There is the power of success and resonance, and there is the power of what seems like failure and resistance. Is connecting with Spirit complicated? With many moving parts? We like to call it — never a dull moment. There is never an end to the promise of communication, always the offering of a new day, a new piece of the puzzle, a deeper connection. Allow that it is lovingly offered and forever available, within reach and within every choice you make without end. It never is "not happening." So never stop seeking, healing, listening, and talking to us.

I asked, "What about the contrast like when it's so easy? You pop in loudly and clearly. When that happens, is something particularly in alignment or what?"

It is our Gift. Allow, receive and be grateful as they come.

If it appears to not be happening, don't doubt the drought. Know that quiet times are not because you are not worthy, or you are not doing things right. Don't let that make you a non-believer. It could just be a matter of timing, or maybe you just need a rest from it. Enjoy the break with no worries that you are losing time, losing vibration, or losing your place.

Use the Tools

There are layers and steps, and plenty of tools to help us all communicate with Spirit. Going back to the fundamentals helps, like remembering who we are as spiritual beings. It helps to make the effort to use and heighten our power tools of intuition and other perceptive modes. It takes practice to learn the language of Spirit, to experience how connecting feels, and to become more comfortable in the vicinity of conversing with other species and other dimensions. These are all steps in the process.

We have tools that help along the way, tools to support and enhance the energy anatomy of who we are, tools to help us practice what we learn, and tools for sustaining our new awareness and transformation. Developing our knowledge about the tools, using, and integrating them will help our next steps to communication.

Some tools are for cleansing and balancing your energy anatomy, some for assisting in raising or maintaining vibration. Some tools take you to a relaxed, more receptive and quiet place for healing, and some are great hands-on instruments to carry in your pocket or put out on the table. Consider using these:

- Reiki, Self-Reiki, Vibrational Healing, Quantum Touch, Ayurvedic medicine, Associative Awareness Technique, Energy Codes, and other modalities of energy medicine
- Homeopathy, massage, acupuncture, hypnosis, and reflexology
- Astrology, kinesiology muscle testing, craniosacral therapy, meridian clearing, chi balancing, chakra balancing, aura cleansing, and aura photography
- Yoga, Tai Chi, movement meditation, qigong, hands-on healing, and tapping
- Crystals, pendulums, pyramids, merkabas, candles, magnets, feathers, sage or incense
- Runes, oracle cards, aromatherapy, and calming music

- Ayurvedic medicine, bio-energy work, sound healing, and all forms of meditation
- Journaling and Automatic Writing

From the list, choose activities and treatments that you enjoy. Spend time with them and with other people who also enjoy using and sharing them. These tools will help you get into the vicinity of hearing and connecting, all part of a transformative journey that comes with layers of healing and a developing relationship with your spirit and your God. Here are more ideas to choose from which I have found to be inspiring.

Inspiration For Communication
- Learn about energy work. Receive energy therapy.

- Create space and time for communicating with Spirit.

- Let go of conventional communication.

- Listen to them and talk to them in *their* language which is the language of the senses.

- Communicate through your heart.

- Be quiet, present, and allow your perceptions to expand.

- Softly focus with Spirit, feel the presence.

- Tune in to the resonance.

- Don't worry about what other people will think.

- Focus on the essence of the moment and why you are there wanting to talk.

- Manifest a moment of connection with humble gratitude for the experience.

- Follow your internal GPS. You'll get there. Or stop and ask for help along the way when you need it from a human mentor, or from Spirit.

- Two great resources you have are attention (awareness) and intention (your goal).

- Your new default of awareness is your power to choose mindfulness.
- Awareness is the portal to living in the present moment.

- We get to invite Spirit communication because we have free will.

- We are privileged to ask because we get to co-create the connection.

- Intend to be in the flow.

- What you are good at is getting better. Yes, it does take practice.

REIKI: What is Reiki? How does it work?

My communication with Spirit benefited from taking Reiki classes and receiving attunements, placements, and ignitions. The power from the healing opportunities plus the Light from inviting Reiki into my life was like a new software that initiated transformation and brought about changes including new pathways to my psychic self and Spirit communication.

Reiki is foremost a treatment modality for relaxation. Being in a relaxed state triggers the body's natural healing. The body wants to heal itself. The basic technique used is referred to as "hands-on holistic healing" and is done by the practitioner using light hand placements above the body, most often above energy centers called chakras. In this fashion, the universal energy that is around us gets directed to the body's chi. The flow of the chi is what helps the body balance and heal.

The treatment session is comfortable and relaxing. You lie on a table fully clothed, or sit in a chair, or remain in a hospital bed and the Reiki practitioner will use various hand movements and light touch on or above your body which focuses the energy. Clients feel the calming sense of healing. It is from this state of being that healing can take place on many levels.

The Reiki treatment can stand alone as therapeutic in itself, or it can work together and complement other medical interventions. Either way, Reiki can help every known illness or ailment with holistic benefits physically, emotionally, and spiritually.

Reiki and Energy Medicine
Reiki is one of over sixty modalities of "Energy Medicine" which are based on the scientific principles of frequency and resonance. Energy medicine recognizes that our cells, tissues, organs and our whole state of being is simply energy at the core, and that energy responds to energy treatments working according to the principles of biology, physics, and transference of energy. The empowering concept underlying the science and techniques is the understanding that you can activate and support your body's natural healing processes.

Reiki energy, spiritually guided energy that is intentionally focused for healing purposes, travels at a healing frequency through the hands of the practitioner, through the receiver's energy anatomy centers and pathways, and through the whole body expanding to the receiver's surrounding aura. The energy can even fill the room. That entire healing space fosters self-healing for the receiver as well as the giver, the client as well as the practitioner, and works through all layers of who we are.

There are many individual testimonies of positive results from applying Reiki, all of which speak to the value of it. Equally compelling are scientific studies that support what happens through the Reiki touch, how, and why it works. The pulsing field of energy produced by the hands of a Reiki practitioner is measurable, and so are the bio-magnetic fields that induce a current of energy in tissues and cells.

Research shows that these various frequencies of energy can aid in nerve regeneration, bone growth, repairing muscle tissue, healing ligaments, calming skin issues, and strengthening capillaries. There is evidence of healing for all types of injuries and diseases, including the most difficult to diagnose and remedy. There are also fascinating conclusions about the Reiki impact on human DNA and the positive power of that.

Healing is not only at the symptom level of disease and injury but importantly at the root causes. The body's healing processes activated by energy medicine address those causes holistically. Those healing actions continually seek to harmonize and balance chi. That effects body, mind, and spirit. Therefore, in addition to physical changes, there are positive changes in a person's state of mind and sense of well-being. There may be healing of emotions, trauma, and relationships. There is development of positive personality traits such as patience, acceptance, gratitude, clarity, and peace.

When we think of ourselves holistically, we know we are physical, emotional, mental, and spiritual beings. We are also energetic beings with an energy anatomy. It is helpful to know what makes up our energy anatomy so we can attend to clearing, balancing, strengthening, and nurturing it.

Our Energy Anatomy
The three main parts of our energy anatomy are meridians, chakras, and our aura. Meridians are the circulatory system for the energy, chakras are the transformers, and our aura is that invisible field of

energy around the physical body that expresses the output of our energy system. Each of these anatomical components have been understood and addressed for years, particularly in eastern medicines like acupuncture, Ayurveda, and others. From those practices, the evidence shows that the body responds to energetic attention and care. When these parts of our energy body are open and working in harmony, the body is able to respond with its best health and from a state of balance.

The meridians, chakras, and aura work together in concert, with the central coordination coming from the chakras. Humans and animals alike have chakras that are identified by name and where they are located on the body. We have at least seven major chakras and as many as twelve along with several minor ones. Regardless of the number, the chakras are vital.

Chakras are interconnected with each other as a system, when one is impacted, you influence the chakras above and below it as well. Individual chakras affect the chi in specific areas of the body with its corresponding physical body systems, organs and tissues. Each one also relates to mental, emotional, and spiritual areas of life like security, relationships, creativity, intuition, and spiritual connection. So when you impact one, the influence is holistic.

There are ways to see and measure the chakra energy centers. They each have a corresponding color, a particular frequency, and a tone value associated with them. Since we all have perceptive modes, any of us at some point may see the colors of the chakras or feel the energy from them. Reiki practitioners may use that to benefit the Reiki treatment. With practice, you can feel when a chakra is open and functioning well which promotes health, or blocked and stagnant which may preclude disease. It is a diagnostic tool to direct the Reiki energy.

What do chakras do? Chakras, like fans, spin energy causing it to funnel like a cone from outside of the body narrowing tightly to a point of contact with the body. These spinning wheel powerhouses draw in universal energy, transmute it to an energy form that the body can use for what it needs, and deliver it to the life force chi. This process fuels the chi to keep it flowing to deliver the vitality we need for health and well-being.

An interesting tool that responds to and demonstrates the spinning direction and radius of energy over a chakra is a pendulum. With the pendulum, chakras can be assessed as open, balanced, sluggish, over-working, or blocked. Knowing the state of the chakras is information the Reiki practitioner can use during the treatment. Not only does it help the practitioner know which chakras to work on, but it gives evidence of the bigger picture and can help show what is behind illness symptoms in order to understand the true causes of physical issues. When our chakras and subsequently any part of our energy anatomy is out of balance, that can become the genesis of disease or illness from headaches to cancers.

A Reiki or energy medicine practitioner can help a client, or a people can discover for themselves which chakras need attention. That awareness is an important place to start the journey of healing. Besides the Reiki treatment, much can be done to cleanse, open, balance, maintain, and energize the chakras, and this is vital to the health of the entire energy anatomy. The chakras are important centers on their own, plus they are interconnected with each other and with the other parts of the energetic system, so the balancing of one affects the others. Chakras are our energetic cores, the go-betweens for the outer body's aura and the inner body's meridians. Working with them promotes healing for the whole body.

Reiki Now
Reiki has been misunderstood in the past, but the benefits are now appreciated more than ever. Originating in Japan, the history is an interesting story of courage, discovery, and calling. It has grown to be used worldwide in a variety of settings including hundreds of hospitals

in the United States and countries around the world. Reiki practitioners and teachers can be found on every continent. There are a variety of lineages and schools of Reiki, practitioners, and associations, and it can be learned by anyone of any age. Helpful tools particular to Reiki include the Five Reiki Precepts, Reiki symbols, hand placements, ignitions or attunements, and various specialized techniques.

Like many energy medicine modalities, Reiki has grown from mainstream alternative medicine to becoming a sought after treatment for all its benefits. And the benefits are not limited to human beings. Animals and plants respond well, and in fact respond with enthusiasm. Every living thing and all types of issues, medical and otherwise, can be positively impacted by Reiki energy.

Look up Reiki practitioners in your area for a treatment or to attend a class. Reiki has been taught to people of all ages and backgrounds all over the world. Find a Reiki master and they can lead you through the levels of classes which are Level I, II, and III which is advanced Reiki training and master teacher level. The most familiar Reiki healing system is called Usui Reiki Ryoho or simply Usui Reiki. You may discover Karuna Reiki® and Levels of Holy Fire initiated by William Rand, or many other styles of Reiki worth looking into.

Intuitive Reiki
One important note to make, particularly in the context of this book, is that there is a distinction between a Reiki treatment and a psychic reading. I am not a trained psychic or medium, and I do not have a practice of giving psychic or medium readings. Nor would any Reiki practitioner need to become a trained psychic or medium. Reiki in its purest form is simply a transference of energy to promote relaxation and healing.

For me, there is a distinction between a Reiki treatment and the sessions I have described in this book when I received messages from Spirit. I offer Reiki Sessions, and I offer Intuitive Reiki Sessions. At first they were one in the same until I learned more about intuitive guidance and about hearing "messages." Now I understand the service to be two different offerings. I am trained with several classes and levels of Reiki, and I am trained with several experiences of learning about and working with intuitive energy, so I offer both.

A person learning Reiki does not need to be trained to offer both. There need not be any pressure ever to "receive information" or "intuitive hits." There could be a beautifully orchestrated cross-over effect, but there is no necessity to offer both.

Being spiritually guided as a Reiki practitioner is valuable, and it is helpful to deliberately ask for guidance and be open to receive it. Using the technique of gassho prior to giving a treatment is encouraged and includes asking for help from spiritual masters. Reiki by definition is a spiritually guided energy, so it is likely that Reiki practitioners will receive information intuitively for the Reiki treatment. With practice, this guidance will come with more clarity, and practitioners will become more confident in using hand placements and techniques that are directed by a divine source. That intuitive guidance is a powerful and holy resource to appreciate.

Simply understand and remember that while intuitive knowing, visions, or hearing from Spirit will be helpful as guidance for the Reiki treatment and the needs of the client, they need not become specific "messages" or information to be told to a client. Clients may not want to receive messages, especially if their expectations are purely to receive healing and balancing from the Reiki energy.

Outcomes of Reiki treatments are best left up to the Reiki energy and our spiritual resources. Those outcomes will be perfect and powerful without a practitioner sharing anything more than simply hands-on healing.

Outcomes of Reiki in my own life have included development of my sixth chakra with its intuitive powers. The gifts that emerged from that evolution of stronger perceptions brought with it the responsibilities of having them. Intuitive guidance for intuitive Reiki comes with a sacred responsibility to use the connection with Spirit respectfully, to honor its Source, to see the Oneness of all living things, and to humbly respond with courage and uprightness to the call to be of service.

Whatever our gifts and talents are, whatever the combination of them is that we use in service, we will all be raising the consciousness of the planet. That is our hallelujah.

Automatic Writing

Writing in a journal didn't start out as a favorite tool of mine, but it is now because it brings such magnificence into my life. All journaling is a personal process whether you create a gratitude journal, family history journal or your own diary. Automatic writing is a type of journaling and personal tool for communication with Spirit. Different than the Evidence Journal which is for writing down to record confirmations and faith builders, it can still be done in the same journal book.

Automatic Writing is about communicating with Spirit in a writing format. As with any journaling, you can be brutally honest and ask all the questions you want. The difference is that you deliberately ask expecting an answer, you deliberately listen to write down what Spirit has to say, and the writing feels like it is happening automatically just like any flowing conversation would. You know it is not you creating the responses, it's Spirit having a conversation.

The phrase "automatic writing" feels more robotic to me than my actual experience, but it is a good way to explain what happens. Your journaling time becomes more than just you writing down your thoughts, your journaling becomes a conversation. It's like a brain storming session with back and forth questions and answers, and you are the participating secretary.

Once the conversation has already begun in you with your believing, quieting, listening, asking, trusting and writing, then you notice that something more is coming into your awareness. It feels like ideas emerge out of a fog, or the development of solutions pop in like the proverbial lightbulb that lights up. You find yourself asking, "Where did that come from?" And then you write, "Where did that come from?" and you hear an answer.

Your part is your thoughts and questions, Spirit's part is answers and guidance. Spirit's part can feel automatic because it has a mind of its own. It works without you thinking about it. You know it's not your idea. No way would you have thought of that third alternative. Your part continues as Spirit uses your experiences and vocabulary to translate the energies of the thoughts, images, feelings, smells, and tastes. Sometimes Spirit uses words you never knew. Then it's fun to look them up and get a new understanding.

It's a good thing you are writing it all down because it will become an adventure to look back on with encouragement and answers direct from Spirit that you will cherish. You won't want to forget the messages that move you and inspire you, so by all means get it down in writing.

It is channeling.

When we use automatic journaling, just like our other means of communication, we get to convey thoughts and translate feelings that come from another dimension, bring messages from the Other Side. That's channeling.

Before you say "no" to channeling, and I know some of you will bristle at the thought because of some negative press, remember that Spirit has been channeling with humans for eons. Not only are many sacred texts channeled from God, which by the way have stood the test of time in their validity and standards, but also the inspirations for much more have been channeled from God who is Spirit. The scientific discoveries, the muses for enlightening poetry, the motivation and inspirations for creating something never known before are all channeled creativity.

When people say, God led me or God spoke to me, it's channeling. Ask people in the creative arts about their moments of inspired painting, photography, and dance. Or ask preachers in their sermon preparation, or Light Workers in their inspired moments of witnessing healing. That energy, that guidance, direction, and motivation is channeled. When you know it all came through you from somewhere else, you are channeling. When you have a knowing that the synchronicity you just experienced was hand-delivered by God, you are channeling.

If you think channeling is not relevant or spiritual, that's a myth. With today's channellings we get a fresh version and updated look at the sacred. We get another chance to hear the Truth through the humans that God chooses to use to bring messages for the benefit of all humanity. Spirit is still helping us and loving us with constant gifts of communication between humanity and divinity.

Be assured that channeling is not a take-over, occult-like, mysterious or shadowy. Quite the contrary, it feels like my closest encounters with God and Spirit ever. It's amazing that Spirit makes the effort to communicate with us and uses our 3D language in order to do so. Spirit could use the scary thunderbolt technique or the parting of the seas if they wanted.

More often, Spirit chooses a loving approach and comes quietly and softly to us where we are. Spirit comes in a way that works for us in our limiting human existence. Spirit channels through us in telepathic conversations through any of our senses, or in written conversations like journaling. It's simply transferring information.

How channeling works for me.

Sometimes I start the process by taking a pen and journal in hand and start writing. Other times I get the nudge or hear the buzz and know that Spirit has something to say. One time I was walking into my office and heard loudly and clearly, "Get your paper and pen because I have something to tell you!"

To get started, I put myself in a receptive mode by going to a quiet place. I start writing in my journal often with a question for Spirit. I write, "Dear Spirit, Sharyn here." then I write the question(s). I put my pen down and listen. Spirit is around me, I can tell. I begin to hear words and thoughts, or feel feelings and sensations.

Sometimes it is a word-by-word process, like on a need-to-know basis, one word at a time. Other times I see an image or sense feelings and look for the words that describe it. That becomes the message. Either way, there's a moment where both Spirit and I are searching for the words in my vocabulary to match what Spirit wants to convey. For me, that's the work of the process. Finding the words. As the channeling unfolds, I can feel the effort on the part of Source as consideration is made to find the best word. Every now and then Spirit comes up with a word I've never heard of so I just go with the flow and look it up later.

Those words become sentences, then sentences into paragraphs. I often have no idea where the writing is going, but I just keep putting the words on the paper. When I write, "And so it is", I

know we are done. Even after it is written, it feels like each word has more depth than simply its literal meaning. Each re-reading can evolve with another layer of meaning upon another. That's the way of Spirit.

Sometimes I feel so tired at that point that I simply fall asleep. Or the opposite happens because I may be wound up at the magnificence of feeling Spirit's presence and knowing that Spirit has been speaking. What makes it stunning and humbling at the same time? It's the magical meld of me, my vocabulary, and my experiences mixing with the sacred allowing of joining with a higher consciousness.

Experiences To Try: Get started with journaling

Start your journaling with whatever feels good to write about. Ask yourself the question, "What gives me joy?   Or...what nurtures my soul?" Think about it, start writing, and more ideas will come.

Or start writing with this: What question would you ask Spirit?   Or choose a specific spirit identity to talk to and what question would you ask if they were right here having a conversation? What would you be saying to each other?   Write down what you wonder about.   Even mystical thoughts like, "I want to access skills from my DNA.   Is that possible?"

When I have a specific question for the Spirit, I begin this way: I write: "Dear Spirit," I would love to hear from you about...."

Think through your question and how you phrase it. I recommend avoiding the "Should I do so and so" questions. When I ask those, I usually hear back the same answer which is, "Well what do you *want* to do?" I can't tell you how many times I've heard that. The "Should I do so and so" questions aren't as effective as when I re-phrase it. For example: "I'm in a quandary about ...this way or that.   What other options would be for my highest good?" Sometimes in response to my "Should I do so and so" asking, Spirit reminds me to let go of the should thinking and consider asking myself, "If there were no limitations, what would I do? If money was not an issue, what would I do? What do I want?" Food for thought.

Experiences To Try: Practice active listening

Listening skills are acquired skills from practicing.   How do you listen? Actively and without judgment? Are you able to listen to every word or are you busy conjuring up your defense? Do you ever repeat what the person is saying to confirm that you are understanding them correctly?   Whatever conversation comes up next today, notice your listening skills. You will want good listening skills for listening to Spirit.

Get to the Talking

You know the basics, and you know you can pre-pave the path and increase your chances of being receptive by developing your spirituality, intuition, imagination, and telepathy. You know how to discern that it is Spirit talking, and you know about the language. You are comfortable with it not happening as you expect, and you have a list of tools for assistance. So let's get to the talking.

Step One: Create the Space

Create a space of quiet, however you want your sacred space to be. Clear the space by smudging, prayer, or Reiki symbols. Burn sage, light a candle, play crystal bowls, play soft music. Use your essential oils and crystals to amplify a connection with Spirit.

Step Two: Grounding

Grounding comes from literally putting your feet down flat on the floor and being aware of the floor beneath you and the earth beneath that, like having magnetic blocks on your feet that hold you down. We need grounding to be centered. To make it part of your spiritual practice, you may want to say a mantra first thing in the morning. Call it your own Centering practice.

"Spirit, help me today to be grounded, centered, and protected
while living out my purpose today."

There are many ways to ground. Most importantly, simply feel your feet on the ground, take a moment to breathe deeply, and on the exhale feel yourself relax into the solid earth. Take another breath and on the inhale feel yourself draw up energy as a gift from Gaia earth. Notice the breath brings awareness to the moment.

Step Three: Cleansing and Peace

Create peace within yourself through intentional breathing, meditation, chanting, Reiki symbols, getting on your knees in prayer, smudging yourself or asking an Archangel to help cleanse your energy field and balance your chakras.

Intentionally let go of worries or doubts. Ask for help to clear what keeps you trapped such as old tapes, fear, guilt, shame, or anxiety. Delete what you don't want. Feel yourself stepping into your power and divine purpose.

Drop into your heart space. Put your hands over your heart, right over left, to help focus your attention there. Send love and be receptive to receive love. Feel and share your gratitude. That'll take you directly to your heart. Stay there. Love from there, feel from there, breathe from there. As you breathe, expand your energy out from your body, past your chair or room, past the house, your country, this planet, this galaxy. By expanding from your heart center outward, you are elevating your consciousness.

Step Four: State Your Intention

State your intention which at first may be for clearing, for clarity, or to meet and communicate with Spirit. State your intention for the highest good of all. Reiki practitioners may stand in gassho and ask for divine intervention to guide the treatment. Ask for Light to unlock awareness of who you are, and LIGHT for sacred expansion. Invite the presence of Spirit. Address a specific identity or address them all. Step into your power and divine purpose.

If you want to use Guided Imagery, especially as a beginner, play a meditation audio. There are specific meditations that take you to a place in which you could meet your Guide, or use any meditation that takes you to a quiet place. Use one of the meditations provided at the end of this chapter.

Step Five: Be Still

Listen. Be still. Breathe. Know you are connecting to Light and Peace. Check to make sure you are not trying too hard. Relax and allow.

Start the conversation. Speak out loud or in your mind, whatever feels most comfortable.

See "Conversation Starters" below to assist you in getting started.

At some point you may <u>feel</u> Spirit's presence, <u>see</u> it, or <u>know</u> it, whatever perceptual mode works for you. Trust. The conversation will be your personal experience. Remember that sensory impressions will come through your inner being, not "at" you. You are connecting to a celestial energy that can transform and transmute. You are a co-creator with Source. Express your appreciation.

Step Six: Settle and Ground Again

When the energy lightens and you sense the end of the conversation, breathe again to connect with your center and the present moment. Notice your feet, notice the room, and notice what is around you. Gently open your eyes.

Take with you the reminder to be extraordinary because you have been in the presence of extraordinary. You have seen, heard, felt and known the communication of Spirit. You may want to journal about your experience, and share with a friend not only the incredible wisdom you have been given but also share that Spirit exists and is eager to communicate with and help us all.

Conversation Starters

Start with your intention, what you want and hope for. Then listen. If it is a Spirit Guide, Angel, or Guardian who you want to have a relationship with, you may want to ask to meet them. Ask them to tell you something about themselves, their name, their strengths. Perhaps they have a gift for you.

If it is a question you have, ask. When possible, leave questions on sensitive or tricky issues until you feel more practiced with connecting, unless it feels urgent. Ask them, "What would it take for such and such to happen?" Some questions might be about your journey. "What am I trying to know the truth of? What am I trying to discover? What repeating tape from my childhood am I not letting go of? Am I asking the right question?"

Go with an issue that is important to you. "I'd love some feedback about...or can you give me insights about...". Or jump right in talking about how you feel, and where you hurt.

You can also ask Spirit for a confirmation. Ask them for a symbol or a color or a word.

Enjoy the conversation. As it comes to a close, thank Spirit. Spend time in appreciation and gratitude. Know that there can always be more conversations. They are always available.

Call to Action: Integrate the Message
Sprinkled within your life will undoubtedly be days of discouragement. On those days, borrow the faith the comes through in this book, trust the evidence from these stories. Put a sticky note on the pages that will remind you that what Spirit has to offer is out of this world, and you will not find it in any other way than through your awareness of Spirit within you, within your community of Light, and within our Multiverse.

On the days you feel glorious, your service will feel light and fulfilling. Enjoy the hallelujah of resonance, alignment, and connection. That comes from integrating all of who you are, integrating who you are with the holy resources available to you. Integrate the conversations and messages of Spirit to pad the lining of your challenging earth journey, to help you live your best life ever.

Take the Steps to Connect: A Reference Sheet

- Learn about Spirit: their ways, their voice, their language, their service to you.
- Be in the vicinity by attending to your spirituality and perception modes.
- Do the work, take the steps, get comfortable, be the vibration.
- Seek Spirit. Listen to your heart.
- Invite the conversation. Accept their invitation.
- Build your relationship. Ask the hard questions. Be open to receive.
- Practice communication. Get to know them better.
- By intention, collect the confirmations, synchronicities, and faith builders.
- Create a journal of those Faith Builders. Create a journal of your communication.
- Collect your favorite affirmations. Post them, chant them, memorize them.

Take care of you.

- Create a daily spiritual practice. Include cleansing, praying, inviting, healing, giving, receiving.
- Work the process for what you want and need.
- Pay attention to how you are feeling.
- Notice blockers, choose enhancers.
- Detox. Let go of what you don't want.
- Reach for higher thoughts and vibration.
- Fill inner spaces with Love and Light.
- Embrace your friends and family.
- Ask for and be open to receive the community of like-minded seekers and healers.
- Choose your service.
- Choose your joy with what fills you up.
- Play with your creativity. Color outside the lines if you want.
- Enjoy the rest periods that come.

Take time to practice.

Integrating spirituality, perceptual gifts, and communicating with Spirit takes its own time. So take your time. Practice allowing, mindfulness, and listening. Practice communication. You may see and feel more than you could imagine, or you may feel nothing at times. That is how it works. Keep evolving. Spirit is with you for the duration.

Practice resting. Go back to your stone. Sit there and rest. Watch for the Ascended Master to come around the corner and sit with you, just to be with you. When you are ready to move again, know that Spirit will boost you when you want to climb, catch you if you happen to fall, and jump for joy with you when you decide to run in your gallop and leap across the precipice.

Take on the service and enjoy the hallelujah.

Do it for yourself, the animals, and the planet.
Witness the Light. Turn on the Light. Be the Light.
A few lights allow all to see better.

Wear the mantle of living your purpose. Enjoy the service. Help in humanity's healing. Display the tapestry. Pat yourself on the back. Count your blessings. Let the sacred messages become your light posts and your wisdom, your affirmations of your truth. Raise the consciousness.

I love the part when I wake up and don't feel anxiety. I love when I see the synchronicities. I love the resonance and the goosebumps to confirm what I know with absolute certainty. I love the moments when I can finally feel the Oneness of all living things and love with God. I love seeing potential being fulfilled and possibilities being embraced with all the power behind belief in the promises.

On the way to learning the art of communication, we realize there is a challenges for growth but never an end to the journey. It's quite the trip to find your means for seeing the invisible and hearing the inaudible.

Spirit communication has been in the land of the mystics for a long time, but we hope it becomes a household phenomenon to talk about Spirit and talk with Spirit. What an eternal investment to teach our children from a young age what it means to "check in with your Spirit." How valuable to apply Spirit messages for the peace they bring to our homes. How priceless to be the Light that brings it all to the world stage.

Anyone may choose to lighten their path and delight their soul by making the effort to communicate with Spirit. Above all else, remember that God and Spirit hear every thought of prayer, and every yearning of the heart.

Do not worry about getting it absolutely right. No steps or procedures need to be followed precisely. Most importantly, show up and talk. Use what you know, apply truth that resonates, and enjoy the journey. It is more about all the bits and pieces of your continuing evolution and your tapestry that create links between the earth plane and other dimensions. Blessings to you for your willingness to seek out and engage with your Spirit team. It helps us all to see your light, experience your service and gifts, and feel your joy.

STAY TUNED…your life is unfolding just as it is meant to be.
You are a diamond and a Light. Sparkle On!

Meditation for Connecting

You may want to play soft music or light a candle. Sit comfortably.
Relax, breathe easily.
Start with Grounding. Put your feet on the floor.
Feel the earth, claim it as your foundation.
Close your eyes if you would like. Invite Spirit to join you.

State Your Intentions such as:
> To disconnect with your outer world; to voyage inward.

To cleanse and balance your energy anatomy.
To welcome communication.
To clearly perceive love, hear, know, and see.
To let go of restrictive thoughts and preconceived notions.
To welcome the help of Spirit for more sensitivity to receiving.
To meet your Spirit Guide.
To have a conversation, to ask questions, to learn more, to
know more.

Put your attention on your breathing and use exhalation to relax deeper until you are fully present and totally relaxed.

Put your hands on your solar plexus, right over left. Breathe into your hands softly and deeply to center yourself.

Visualize yourself immersed in light. Visualize a golden light washing over your crown, moving to cover your whole body. Say, "Bless me with divine healing rays."

Using the "Four Breaths" techniques, breathe in and out four times, each time focusing on these four thoughts:

- Breathe to ground yourself, breathe up from the earth.
- Breathe for cleansing, clearing, letting the light reach in and through to cleanse every cell.
- Breathe to calm your mind, with the exhale release your thoughts, worries, anxieties, fears.
- Breathe through your heart. Drop into your heart, put your focus there, connect there.

You may want to move your hands to put them on your heart to bring your attention there, right over left. Breathe through your heart front and back. Notice: Do you feel open and peaceful? Breathe softly until you are there.

Now connect with your inner world through your mind's eye. If you see green in your mind's eye, green is the frequency of the heart and healing.

Be present for healing as Divine light touches you, effortlessly heals, allows you to forget about fears, resentments, anger, mistakes, worries. Allow yourself to accept this healing, this love, this light. Give thanks for wellness, love, and balance.

Breathe now through your crown. If you see purple, this is the color of the frequency of your third eye chakra and your 193. Ask for help from your Guides and from God to balance your spirituality, your awareness of God, and to help you develop awareness of your psychic abilities, increase your mindfulness, and to learn to trust your instincts and your inner voice.

Know that Spirit is with you and in your presence. With intention, send love from your heart to the Spirit identity you have called in. If it is your Spirit Guide you want to meet, sense your love to them, theirs to you. Connect Heart-to-Heart.

Invite Spirit to talk with you. When you are connected, impressions will come. Notice your feelings, watch for pictures, be open to smells or tastes, listen for words.

It may help to send thoughts or questions like these:

Introduce yourself. Express your gratitude to meet with them.
Ask about them, who they are, do they have a name, do they have a message for you. Ask them any questions you have. Ask them to help you hear.

They may have a gift for you or offer you a word, a feeling, or a message. Thank them for caring for you and being with you.

At some point, the energy will lighten and fade as your time comes to an end. Know you can visit with them again at any time.

Consider this benediction: Thank you for giving me an intuitive connection with the divine. Thank you for access to higher beings that honors prayer and communication. Thank you for sacred gifts. Thank you for allowing me to be of service to others, to be an earth angel. Thank you for the opportunity to be a bridge to understanding and love between all species on the planet.

Today's miracle: We can communicate with Spirit as we see with our mind's eye, hear with our heart, and feel with our soul.

Bring your thoughts into the present. Notice the room around you, notice your feet on the floor. Breathe in appreciation. Slowly open your eyes. When you are ready, make sure your feet can feel the ground. Take in the experience, meditate a few moments about what you hear, saw, and felt. Write your thoughts down in your journal.

Meditation for Clearing with the Archangels

This is an example of a meditation for clearing your energy anatomy with the help of the Archangels. As with all meditation experiences, create a quiet place for it. Light a candle or incense, or play quiet music. Reiki practitioners may want to use symbols for clearing. Do some body stretches, then find a comfortable position to begin the following meditations steps.

- Start with a few deep breaths to slow your heart rate, relax your body, and calm your mind. Notice your natural breathing rhythm.

- Relax your entire body, one breath, one limb, one joint and one organ at a time. Go through them all.

- Lift and lower your shoulders, pulling them up and letting them fall. As you do that again, remind yourself that burdens have no bearing at this moment. Allow what you have been carrying to lift off. Feel your concerns dissolve and disappear. They are not yours now.

- Let your spine clear by stretching it up tall. Keep it straight and erect, then let it relax. Place your palms on your heart or open them facing upwards as they relax to your side.

- Feel the solid ground under your feet. Under you is part of the planet; the earth that grounds you.

- Now settle in. With your eyes closed, you are supported in this quiet place. Take a moment to think of something you are thankful for. Find your place of gratitude. Breath comfortably.

- Visualize light beginning to flow from above your head. See it come down through your spinal channel bringing divine energy to every chakra and every cell all the way down to your feet. Breathe in a way that takes the light all the way through your body. See the light in it's magical way, fan out and become like roots connecting you and holding you firmly to the sacred ground of the earth.

- As you feel those roots supporting you, imagine the light coming back up to you through your feet, fueled by a creative and grounding force, a divine gift from the earth. Deliberately inhale and run energy from the earth up to the top of your head and back down to the earth. Make the exhale deliberate as well so that it leaves through your cells, expanding outward as every cell feels the light and energy flow through them.

- Now let your mind be still. You can safely and comfortably allow your inner voice to calm down. The voice that truly matters right now is the quieted voice of awareness, consciousness, and aliveness. Relax into your willingness to trust, allow, and receive.

- Thank your guardians, guides, and all the Beings of Light for being with you. You have the gift of free will so you could choose otherwise, but you are inviting them to be a part of your meditation time. Invite the presence of Spirit, the identity of God that you most easily connect to, the archangels, the energy of Holy Fire, Jesus, God and other masters of the heavens.

- Breathe deeply and allow yourself to feel the infinite love of the presence of your Spirit Team. It's like a bath in the desert, a sparkling shower on a warm sunny day. There is a waterfall of white light flowing over you.

- Open up your mind's eye as you say to yourself, "I am open to receive whatever it is that I need at this moment in my life."

- Invite the presence of Archangels Michael, Raphael, Gabriel, and Uriel. These Beings of Light fulfill their purpose by being available to humanity, and they want to connect with you.

- Imagine the presence of **Archangel Michael** in the purple colors of your mind's eye. Ask for this: "Help me to pull out the stressful feelings of fear, anger, worry, despair and anything in my body, mind, soul, and aura that is not helpful." Michael calls it <u>psychic debris</u> and knows how to gather it and take it away to be transmuted to positive energy. Then ask him: "Please reverse the flow now and fill up any empty spaces with the golden and white light of healing and love."

- Breathe and allow. As you breathe, imagine it to be so. It is happening with every inhale and exhale. "Thank you, Michael."

- Let your mind's eye be surrounded with the color green. Ask **Archangel Raphael** to help with healing. Visualize Raphael using a magnetic wand which looks like a light saber. Like a magnet, it can pull out what Raphael calls <u>attachment debris.</u> What is that? Raphael says, "Because you are empathic and feeling the energies around you, you can attract debris."

- Ask Raphael, "Help me to love with sacred empathy from my heart. Heal my energy fields and fill my heart and mind with your higher frequencies of thought. Help me to let go of what is not mine.

Saturate my cells with divine love that trusts and knows that all things are as they are meant to be."

- Ask Archangel Raphael to slowly, mindfully, gracefully move that glowing magnetic wand over every part of your body; your cells, your DNA, your heart, feelings, mind, and soul. Imagine all attachment debris going into that magic wand to be transmuted to light and love.

- Breathe and allow. Say, "Archangel Raphael, fill me with Light and Love. Thank you, Raphael."

- See the yellow, golden light of **Archangel Gabriel** stepping in. He is a healer of <u>message debris</u> which are old messages about not being safe, not being worthy. Ask Gabriel, "Please heal one more layer of what has piled up in my body, mind, and soul. I allow your touch to be the force that nullifies and melts away old, painful messages. Bring to my mind your message of truth about who I really am. Help me to feel the love of the Universe."

- Ask Archangel Gabriel to remove message debris. Declare it gone. Ask Gabriel, "Give me a new message; a new mantra. Remind me that I am enough. I have all I need. My peace is my strength. With the power of your yellow golden light, touch every part of me, every cell of me, with the strength of Light, the confidence of purpose, and the peace of co-creating with my ego and co-creating with my fellow light workers. Thank you Gabriel."

- Breathe and allow.

- Within the white light, **Archangel Uriel** is with you. She has been healing <u>trauma debris</u>. If you are familiar with Reiki symbols, she invites you to use the CKR symbol on your chakras. If you are not familiar with that, say to yourself and your entire being, "By Divine Decree, I am healed." Healing, protection, fulfillment of purpose, and all that you need comes from your connection with your own divinity which strengthens your connection to your Source. That is a truth you can stand on.

- Ask Archangel Uriel to dissolve all trauma debris, one layer today, and another one tomorrow. By Divine Decree, allow it to be.

- Say, "Archangel Uriel, strengthen my connection to Source. I want to be in alignment. I want to recognize resistance so I can let it go and come back to Center. Touch me with your sacred white light to strengthen my channel to the Divine. I allow and step into an expanded life having been touched by Spirit. Thank you, Uriel."

- Breathe and allow. And so it is.

- Feel your gratitude. Feel the balance, the grounded-ness, the hope, and the inspiration from renewal. Come back to the earth plane again.

- Be aware of your body and the space around you. With a heavenly sigh, touch base with your feet on the floor, your body in the room. Slowly open your eyes and take in the healing stillness.

Spirit eagerly wants us to rely on them as
available and accessible Beings of Light.
Spirit wants us to remember who we are as divine
perceptual beings, and to know that we can cross the
dimensions to make the sacred connections.

Epilogue

The *Spirit Speaks* stories come from the human experience with our problems, challenges, pains, and complaints. They reveal how those experiences can be viewed from Spirit's perspective. Spirit gives us insight into the spiritual being of who we are.

The *Spirit Speaks* messages remind us that we are souls with eternal life, and our souls can communicate through dimensions of eternity with Spirit in all its identities and benevolence. The messages give us practical advice and wisdom that when applied support us through our earthly life experience.

Spirit Speaks for me has been an opportunity to experience Divinity. Through the stories, I have more knowing about Spirit and that changes me. From that knowing of who Spirit is and what Spirit offers us, my soul is more content to spend its energy on love, compassion, understanding, kindness, goodness, mercy, acceptance, gentleness, and benevolence.

The more I hear from Spirit, the more it makes sense that life's circumstances and difficulties are ideally suited to bring out the best in each of us as we are challenged to evolve. The Spirit insights bring front and center a renewed awareness that everything is as it is meant to be, and that we can live as Lights in the world with help that is available for the asking.

I've gained from Spirit's wisdom the value in letting some things go. I've let go of repeating tapes in my head that were not helpful anymore. I've kicked to the curb my fears about making a mistake, and I rest in knowing that when I do make a mistake, there is correction to be handled and consequences to work through. That's different from punishment to be endured or self judgment and shame to suffer. From all the Spirit reminders, I get it now that when people give me headaches or when bad things happen, it can all be understood as opportunities to grow.

Most of all, I like focusing on Spirit, reading how Spirit is on our side. Spirit observes all and knows all but is not judgmental. Spirit gives us the time we need to walk our path, to listen and work on becoming the best that we can be. Spirit loves us without needing us to be perfect or have it all together. Spirit loves to connect with us, encourage us and answer our tough questions. And if we are side-tracked, Spirit shines a light to help us get back on track.

Spirit reminds us that we are all One. With this realization, I can express compassion rather than judgement. I can cancel out my complaints and upset because I realize that we are all here on our own journeys. We are equally having our trials for the sake of learning and growing and so at any point, any of us could not be having our best day and not behaving from the place of our higher self. I can give you a pass and hope that you will give me one too, remembering that we can support and help each in cooperation rather than competition, in blessing rather than fear.

I am thankful for the chance to do this work and to share it with you. My prayer is "Dear God, I want this to be Spirit-led, Spirit-fed, Spirit-written, and Spirit-highlighted for the purposes of Lighting the path for us all to breathe the Light and to be comfortably filled up with the essentials of life which are Love and Joy." May it be so.

Afterword: Note from the Author

I love hearing from all identities of God, Spirit, and the Collective of them all. If you do too, you will want to read my other two titles in the **Live In The Light Series** called **The Departed Speak** and **The Collective Speak.** Both are soon to be published. This series of books celebrates that God in all Oneness and all Identities is available, accessible, and eager to serve humanity. God and the Beings of other dimensions want us to know more to illuminate our journey, lighten our load, and be soothed as we explore the expansion of who we are in the multiverse of God and Spirit.

The messages you will read in **The Departed Speak** are written down as I heard them from many departed loves ones. They want us to know what it is like to die and what it is like to live, from heaven's perspective. There is so much to learn from these souls who have accomplished the passing on. They are eager to tell us about it from their place of discovery, excitement, and renewed awareness of the multi-dimensional way of life. They offer us advice for getting through the grief, information to help us recognize the signs they send for our relief, and ideas about how to live while we are still in the earth school.

The messages in **The Collective Speak** are from the collective group of departed souls and Spirit speaking as one. These are loved ones, guides, celestial energies of angelic beings, ascended masters, God and identities of God. They answer the hard questions. We can learn from them, understand, and know for certain that life is sacred and that communication with Spirit is a conversation to behold. They are on our side speaking about the treasures and gifts offered to us for the benefit of all Kingdoms on our planet and in the multiverse.

Enjoy all the messages. Find the resonance of truth in them that can impact how you live and help you sustain the perspective of Spirit who will never let you down. My sacred intention is that these words will be customized by Spirit so that we all receive what we need at this moment in our lives. Highlight those mantras, the encouragement that speaks to you.

My hope is that the messages will guide, inspire, and teach you as they have taught me. I hope that you find help for connecting with God and all identities of God including departed souls in spirit. These connections in turn will help you on your sacred journey this time around, this journey of healing, evolving, and being of service.

I hope these collections give answers and solve mysteries about what we may otherwise have trouble visualizing. May the insights bring encouragement that life is worth the effort and love is worth the cost. May we all remember there are eternal reasons for everything. May you be inspired to practice and develop your innate intuition, continue your conversations with other dimensions, keep in touch with your Spirit Team, and connect with "All That Is." Thank you for seeking and being a part of raising the consciousness of the planet.

Join me in the conversation. Send me your stories of messages from Spirit. Give me your permission to share them and that becomes **Spirit Speaks Messages From Around the World** to further inspire us to seek and know our Spirit. It would help us all wrap our brains around the truth of Oneness that all living things on our planet Earth are One with the universal **Spirit Speaks** of galaxies. Email me at: sharynreiki@yahoo.com.

NAMASTE. The God in me salutes the God in YOU.

About the Author: Sharyn Madison
MS, SCT, RM

Masters of Science in Education, Certified
Educator and Coach
Licensed Aesthetician & Skin Care Therapist
Certified Vibrational Healing Practitioner
Certified & Registered Reiki Master/Teacher
and Practitioner
Usui Holy Fire III and Karuna Reiki® Master
Authorized Provider of LMT CEU credits

Even as a high school student, Sharyn had a passion for teaching and community service. Earning her Master's Degree with dual certification in Education and Physical Education, she was a professional educator and coach in public and private schools for 30 years.

During that same time, she was a workshop speaker for educational and spiritual events including her own workshops called *The Laws of the Learner*. When she wasn't teaching, she participated in trips and international projects such as refurbishing a school in Colombia, building a gym in Guadeloupe, painting a church in the Dominican Republic and teaching English in Thailand.

Sharyn retired from professional teaching in order to focus on owning, managing, and providing services at Invigorations Wellness Center in New York. As a licensed aesthetician and having completed several master classes, she provided skin care therapy services at the Center.

Sharyn added Reiki to her other services as a Master Teacher with advanced training and certifications in both Usui and Karuna Reiki®

Holy Fire III. She has experience with Crystal Healing, Color Therapy, Chakra Balancing, Vibrational Healing, Quantum Touch, Associative Awareness Technique, and Essential Oils.

Sharyn gives Reiki treatments and teaches Reiki classes for all levels, for both Usui and Karuna Reiki®. She is authorized by the professional NCBTMB (National Certification Board for Therapeutic Massage and Bodywork) to give CEU credits to qualified Licensed Massage Therapists. Sharyn at times leads Reiki Share Groups, speaks at Reiki Retreats, and gives informative talks to schools and organizations.

From Sharyn: "I am honored to teach and share healing messages that transform my own life. What a blessing to witness evolution as we all awaken to who we are as spiritual beings. There is always more to experience and learn as citizens of the universe. Now that's a hallelujah."

Email: sharynreiki@yahoo.com
Website: www.sharynmadison.com

Made in the USA
Middletown, DE
17 June 2019